History of Freemasonry in England

Also from Westphalia Press
westphaliapress.org

History of Freemasonry in England from 1567 to 1813

by Leon Hyneman

WESTPHALIA PRESS
An Imprint of Policy Studies Organization

Westphalia Press
An imprint of Policy Studies Organization
1527 New Hampshire Ave., NW
Washington, D.C. 20036
info@ipsonet.org

ISBN-13: 978-1-63391-582-4
ISBN-10: 1-63391-582-4

Cover design by Jeffrey Barnes:
jbarnesbook.design

Daniel Gutierrez-Sandoval, Executive Director
PSO and Westphalia Press

Updated material and comments on this edition
can be found at the Westphalia Press website:
www.westphaliapress.org

HISTORY

OF

FREEMASONRY

IN ENGLAND

FROM

1567 TO 1813,

INCLUDING AN ANALYSIS OF ANDERSON'S CONSTITUTION OF 1723 AND 1738, AUTHORIZED BY THE GRAND LODGE OF ENGLAND.

BY LEON HYNEMAN,

Author of "THE ORIGIN OF FREEMASONRY"; Formerly Editor of "THE MASONIC MIRROR AND KEYSTONE"; Etc., Etc.

NEW YORK:

R. WORTHINGTON, 750 BROADWAY.

1878.

TO

THE CRAFT UNIVERSAL.

———————————

THIS Book is written in the interest of pure, legitimate, Ancient Masonry, and not as a remunerative effort. Its aim is to give direction to Masonic thought in the elimination and expression of the great fundamental principles of the Institution, pure *Universal*, *Cosmopolitan* MASONRY and *Charity*.

To the Freemasons of the Old School this Book will be most welcome, in view of the innovating tendencies changing the character and design of the Institution from its original aims. To these, and all right-thinking Masons, whose minds are imbued with a sense of the responsibilities resting upon them, as children of the Universal Father, to *seek truth*, and to appropriate it, no apology is needed for this production.

This Book is not written in the view of what Masonry is, as expressed in these days, but what it should be, and its design in the fulfilment of solemn covenants assumed by every Freemason. The necessity for its writing will appear in the wide departures from original fundamental principles. It is not

iii

written in the popular Masonic style, to allure the
ignorant and unthinking masses, within and outside
of the Institution, with the belief that Masonry is a
great reformatory school; neither as a propaganda
effort, by specious or seeming sentimental laudation,
to induce the outside masses to seek admission into
the fraternity.

We have a higher aim, and eschew, as a Mason, all
efforts at popularizing Masonry outside of the exemplification of its principles in the upright and useful
lives of its members, their efforts to improve and
benefit their fellow-beings, and exemplifying the great
principles of Charity, divinely illustrated in relief of
poor needy Masons, their widows and orphans.

The popular Masonic writers of the past and present time have created, through their publications, a
literature inimical to every feature and principle of
legitimate Masonry, which, as historical, is mainly
mythical; if traditional, fabulous; if symbolical, sectarian and destructive of universal catholic Masonic
principles. In the aim of sectarianism, legends and
legendary myths pre- and post-Adamic, sculptures on
ancient remains, engravings on ancient coins, paint-
ings, &c., on Monastic and other structures, and ceremonial usages and traditions of savage tribes, are all
eagerly sought and incorporated into what is considered the literature of Masonry, with the view to effect
a popular sentiment favorable to the Masonic Institution upon the public mind, and to impress unthinking
Masons with illusory conceptions of the widespread
antiquity of Masonry, as well as the great learning of
the writers.

The misdirection of the Masonic mind, from causes referred to, and the undue efforts to render Masonry popular, has been the means to create a desire to join the fraternity, and hence the great rush of applicants to be made Masons. The influences to that end are caused more by sectarian innovations than anything else, as the effects are to cause Masons to look lightly upon the Institution, and to weaken the importance of the obligations taken, and the teachings Masonry inculcates.

We are opposed to all sectarian allusion or illustration in Masonry. The substitution of the word Religion, so freely used by Masonic writers, is only a cheat and a fraud, as religion is not meant, but the creed and articles of faith of some sectarian denomination. The word religion is seldom considered in a universal sense, and rarely so by Masonic writers. Its substitution for creed has caused cosmopolitan Masonry to be ignored, and the tendency, since Templarism has been very generally engrafted into the Masonic system, is to narrow Masonry into a particular sect.

We hold that sectarianism has no proper conception of Deity, of God the Universal Father. The natural tendency of sectarianism is to narrow man's conceptions of the Divine Being, and to narrow his relations to his fellow-men. It is inimical to fraternity in a wide sense, and hence foreign and opposed to the universal principles of Masonry. It does not recognize a common brotherhood, neither a common paternity, and follows, even to the grave, the remains of those who are not of the same creed, members of the same church.

Masonry, in its broad, comprehensive view of Deity, comprehending the attributes of omnipotence, omniscience, and omnipresence, recognizes the power, wisdom, and love of God, in the unfoldment of universal nature, the efficient means provided to supply all possible true needs of his children, and that universal humanity are one family, and that all live, move, and have their being in one Universal Parent.

Masonry, therefore, makes no distinction among men, acknowledges all as brothers, but in its aims, as an organization to improve and benefit mankind, confines the association to such only as have the disposition, manifested in their lives, to co-operate in promoting the objects of the Institution. In this effort no distinction nor differences among men are known, as to place of birth, of race, creed, or opinion; but those only of whatever nation are privileged to unite in its useful and beneficent aims who have an established character for integrity, uprightness, love of their kind, and are well known for their efforts in behalf of humanity, and as possessing benevolent dispositions.

The principles of Masonry are practical, and founded upon the basis illustrated by the Divine Being in the phenomenal manifestations of nature, the universal exemplar through which God teaches all human life the mode and manner of his government. All aims are only valuable as they are useful. To be employed in uses should be man's aim in individual or associative efforts. God never intended man to be idle only in rest, to recuperate and renew his energies. Human beings are finite, and subject to nature's limitations, and therefore need rest. God is infinite, and is ceaselessly at work, through the instrumentality of his laws, in unfolding phenomenal nature.

In progressive civilization, man is a co-worker with God. In order, therefore, to be useful in promoting civilization, as God designed he should be, he must exercise his faculties to unfold his interior perceptions. Man can only be useful as he is intelligent, and only in that degree. The more intelligence he has, the greater his capacity for usefulness. Man should therefore exercise his faculties — expand them in increasing knowledge — so that he can more ably co-operate and fulfil the design of the Creator in advancing civilization, and add to the comfort and happiness of his fellow-men.

Masonry should be a great instrumentality in promoting useful knowledge, and conducing to the welfare and happiness of mankind. Such should be its aim, otherwise it is of but little use, and like the non-producer, would only be an impediment to the world's progress. Departing from its original aim, from the fundamental principles upon which the system is based, Masonry has been diverted into a different channel, contrary to its intents, and subversive of its efforts in humanity's cause. It is no longer a co-worker with God in advancing the race. It no longer walks with God the Universal Father. The

God named in connection with religion, in effusions of orators and addresses, is the God of Theology, a contracted being, and not the God of Masonry.

We believe that the principles of Freemasonry, outwrought in their fulness, are the best ever devised by man to promote his happiness in this life and advance him to higher spheres in spirit life. The visible and invisible worlds are all embraced in God's universe. God is a spiritual being. Man is a physical and a spiritual being. The former is subject to the limitations of nature; the latter is not subject to any limitations. It is the spiritual that is the intelligent moving cause of the activities of the physical man.

The spiritual never loses its consciousness. The intelligence it possesses, and all that it has acquired in the development of its individuality, it carries with it into spirit life, and ever continues to develop its individuality in its progress through the eternal spheres. The spiritual is not buried with the physical. Life is eternal. These are the higher teachings of Masonry in their symbolic illustration.

The spiritual is *within* all expressions of man, and all of Nature's productions. Within is the spiritual life — the true life; the outer is only *the manifestation of life*. All objective nature — material and immaterial — are the outwrought *manifestations of life*. Objective nature is outwrought of invisible elements combining according to affinity. The invisible elements aggregate into concrete materiality and are reduced again to elements; the rock and tree, all objective materiality becomes invisible.

Nature's life is in incessant and continual change, in building up forms, in renewing elements from decaying and decomposed materiality. In the ultimate all things become invisible, but there is nothing lost in all of nature's changes. This brief illustration is convincing proof of man's immortality. As nothing is lost in nature, so consciousness the ultimate of God's phenomenal manifestations, God's medium through which man becomes a co-worker with him, can lose nothing that it has acquired in being divested of the material body.

As the consciousness is never in abeyance, and as God works in and through uses only, the spirit life of man must have a purpose; that purpose, as God never works in vain, must be in the unfolding of the consciousness to higher and ever higher attainments. In view of the eternal life, life then in the material form is most important, and not to be trifled with and frittered away in the frivolous manner it generally is. Freemasons, of all men, should give this subject their earnest attention. The subject specially pertains to Masonic teachings. It is illustrated in the ritual work. But the explanations, if adverted to at all, are in accordance with theologic teachings, and hence the dogma of the resurrection of the physical body incorporated by many of the clergy and sectarian religionists in explanation of the subject.

The study of man, the chief and most important of all subjects, erect in form, with commanding figure, is that which Freemasons should give their attention to. It should be all-absorbing. It embraces more

than can be written. In the production of the human
form, all nature, all the elements in lower life, in
lower forms, are concentrated to make up the ultimate of God's works, the human being, dual, man
and woman, forming one complete individuality. All
lower life and forms gradually progress upwards in
harmony with the original aim of divine being to produce the intelligent being formed in God's likeness —
man and woman — the completion of nature's phenomenal productions. How great the theme, sublime
the subject, the consideration that the thought in the
divine mind to create a being formed after his likeness, involved the gradual process through illimitable
ages, to produce the conditions through the fulfilment
of nature's forces in phenomenal manifestations to
attain the grand end in the conscious human being,
appearing on the stage of mundane life! But the
primal process of nature's developments, however
mysterious the subject may appear, and although
science in its progressive movements has done much
to bless and benefit mankind, yet in its investigations
confined to details, has not arrived at a knowledge of
the principles and laws through which phenomenal
nature is outwrought, whilst the infinite mind is constantly illustrating the process to human sensuous
observation.

To the Craft Universal these thoughts are addressed, in the hope that some at least, however few,
may turn their thoughts to the study of themselves,
the aim and object of life, and in the progress of investigation they will not only learn more of the

nature, and attributes, and mode of God's government, but that the study will greatly add to their happiness, and give them the conscious conviction of eternal life and progression in spirit spheres.

In the review of Masonry in England we confined our investigations chiefly to Anderson's two Books of Constitutions and Preston's Illustrations. In our comments we have been plain, outspoken, and severe, which some may consider too much so, but in our judgment the subjects merited all and more than we have expressed. The investigation we considered a duty, and are satisfied with its performance. Although disagreeable the necessity for the task, it was undertaken as a labor of love, and not for any remuneration it might give. The judgment of the Craft was intentionally misdirected by the London Masons in the last century, and, as no one had undertaken to examine and compare the Grand Lodge publications, perhaps, from not having all the editions, or, if so, having read them carelessly; or, from lack of interest, not comparing them to ascertain if they agreed; we considered it necessary to perform the labor, in order to give a right direction to Masonic thoughts.

The quotations, dates, and figures, taken from original copies, may be relied on as correct.

Our review does not take in the Union of the two bodies of Masons, but reaches to the time when it was about being consummated. Although no one can apply our remarks on the conduct of the London Grand Lodge, the members under its banner, or the authors referred to, to the Masons in England since the union, we consider it essential, not to be misunderstood, to say a few words in regard to the present Grand Lodge of England, and will close with the following observations. The influence of one good and true man, by his example, may exert an influence upon others that will extend far and wide, in time and space. The example of the Prince of Wales, in being unbiassed and not entering into the un-Masonic and illiberal feelings of the London Masons, more than his exalted position, had the effect to cause an entire revolution in change of disposition and sentiment, among the London Masons under the Earl of Moira. The influence of his example, in the direction of cosmopolitan Masonry, and adherence to fundamental principles, has extended through all the years to the present time, throughout the entire length and breadth of the extended jurisdiction of the United Grand Lodge of England.

ANCIENT YORK

AND

LONDON GRAND LODGES.

IT is a source of great disappointment to the Masonic student, in his attempts to investigate and satisfy himself as to the probable origin of certain subjects connected with Freemasonry, to find, on looking over the authorized publications and prominent authors, so very little to assist him in his efforts. It is not alone the meagre and insufficient details which characterize all these works which annoy and disgust the student in his researches, but the mortification to discover that important matters in one book, whether of authority or not, are either omitted in others or additional matter introduced not in the original. It is the same in historical data, transactions at Grand Lodge meetings, or current events among the fraternity; and which to accept as the most reliable is very embarrassing, and the course generally pursued is that the attempts end in projecting a theory, as others had before him, on the problematical, dubious, and insufficient data furnished in the authorized Grand Lodge's publications.   That has been uniformly the case, with but few exceptions, of all Masonic historians and writers treating on the subject of Freemasonry in the last one hundred and fifty years.   There is one general thought traversing all these inditings, one direction in which they agree in their ventilations, one central standpoint out of which they do not range, which is, a uniform conformity in agreement with the views of the Grand Lodge publications, as if they were of divine inspiration, and their authority not to be questioned by finite minds.

Dr. Oliver, in his "Account of the Schism" in England, and his elaborate letters on the "Origin of the English Royal Arch," with seemingly the best intentions to be unbiassed in writing to his friend and reverend brother, Dr. Crucifix, yet he wrote as if trammelled and confined in his range of thought to views in accord with all his other Masonic writings.

The first authorized Masonic publications were the Books of Constitutions published by order of the London Grand Lodge in 1723 and 1738 respectively, which were compiled by Dr. Anderson, and of which he claimed to be the author.   Preston published his "Illustrations of Masonry" in 1772.   This book ran through many editions, has been reprinted in many places, is known in every country where Freemasons are found; and although a century has passed since its first appearance, it is still held in high favor as the best history of Masonry by Freemasons generally.   Anderson's Books of Constitutions, although published by direction and with the sanction of the

Grand Lodge and its approval, if they had not been reprinted by others, would scarcely be known by the fraternity at this day, which to a very general extent is the case with particularly the 1738 edition. As Anderson and Preston materially differ in their statements of historical occurrences as well as the passing current events, it seems strange that no person in England has yet attempted to institute a comparison as to the reliability of the statements made by the two authors, wherein they differed as to Masonic events noted by one, and differently stated by the other, or altogether omitted. Preston is decidedly more full and clear than Anderson, although both wrote in the interest of the London Grand Lodge, yet not with the same bias of feeling. Anderson was one of the originators of the London Grand Lodge, and as a man of strong prejudices he was biassed in all his inditings, evidences of which are seen throughout his two publications on every possible occasion, in the omission of historical facts, or giving a contrary construction to, and diverting attention in cases reflecting unfavorably upon the New Grand Lodge. The Books of Anderson, however, are almost universally accepted by the Masonic fraternity as containing a true history of Freemasonry, at least from the time our review commences, and the Ancient Charges, especially those contained in the 1723 edition, are as generally adopted as the fundamental law and basis of Masonic principles. But notwithstanding Anderson's Books of Constitutions were published by order of the London Grand Lodge, with its approval and sanction, yet no more untrustworthy, unreliable books were ever printed under the direction of any organized association. We affirm that Anderson is not to be credited. The Books of Constitutions were written purposely to deceive, to mislead and misrepresent facts as they existed; and if his reports of Grand Lodge Proceedings are true copies of Grand Lodge Records, then the records were corrupted with the design to mislead the reader. That such was the case will be seen hereafter.

The general sentiment favorable to Anderson is mainly because of his compilation of the "Ancient Charges," and because Masons read them without due reflection and accept his statements as authority. That which is popular is not always true. A statement made by an author in regard to an historical event is often misstated in some interest or other to mislead, and this Anderson has done. Dr. Oliver, one hundred years later, in the same manner perverted history to render more probable the misstatements of Anderson. But Dr. Oliver, in his reprint of Preston's Illustrations, notwithstanding his omission of important particulars, has given sufficient evidence of Anderson's unreliability as author and compiler; yet Anderson's Constitutions are the gospels Freemasons swear by. They are accepted as if of divine authority. He is the light which shineth in the darkness to believers. Was he not a minister of the Gospel, and therefore incapable of being biassed against truth in his productions as author?

The history of the organization of the Grand Lodge

in London in 1717, with the reasons stated for the movement, are insufficient, incomplete, and not consistent with Anderson's own statements. The prior movements of the craft in London, as stated by Anderson, conflict with his version of the cause which led to the formation of the Grand Lodge. He differs widely from Preston in important particulars. The movement, without a critical analysis of preceding events showing an object to attain, an ultimate end in harmony with the culmination of the end sought, will be an incomprehensible mystery, and hence the confliction of views of earnest investigators at the present time. The 1717 movement was not a " revival," as Anderson has it, and recent writers contend it to have been. REVOLUTION is the proper term, as it was the culmination of revolutionary movements commenced more than one hundred and fifty years prior, and continued through all those years to gain the end aimed at. The movements subsequent to 1717 prove it, as the course pursued by the new Grand Lodge towards the York Grand Lodge was of the same character as before the revolution. The York Grand Lodge cannot be ignored, as Anderson and some writers of the present day aim to do. It has a record prior to 1717 and subsequent, although Masonry in print prior to 1723 was a rare occurrence.

The 1723 publication is silent as the grave on the subject of the new Grand Lodge,—does not even allude to it, nor mention it in any way, although it contains a history running from "Adam, our first parent," down to " our present worthy Grand Master, the most

noble Prince John, Duke of Montagu." This brought
the so-called history down *five years after* the revolution and the formation of the new Grand Lodge; but
not a word of that important event, no reference nor
allusion to a single incident or circumstance in connection with it,—the subject has no place in that publication. Ominous silence! Were the four Lodges
which met with "some old Brothers" at the Apple-
Tree Tavern without any connection with or relation
to other Masonic organizations? Whence the origin
of the four Lodges? The members must have been
made Masons under some authority. There must
have been some prior organization under whose authority they were received and admitted into the fraternity. Who were those "old Brothers"? Under
what banner were they made Masons? How many
Masons were present at the meeting at the Apple-
Tree Tavern? Anderson gives us no information on
these subjects.

In the 1738 publication, Anderson, in an enlarged
history, gives an account of the formation of the
London Grand Lodge, (which see further on,) from
which it will be seen that the above questions are pertinent and significant. It must be remembered that
Anderson, Desaguliers, and others, who were promot-
ers of the revolution and active members of the new
Grand Lodge, and continued so to at least until after the
approval of the 1738 publication, must have known, as
they were men of education, that the meagre, insufficient, imperfect statement in the 1738 edition would
not and could not be satisfactory to the intelligent

reader of the circumstances connected with the organization of the new Grand Lodge. It would seem that in the interest of truth, and for future information and reference, the details of organization would have been published; the notice or circular calling the meeting, with the object stated to be accomplished, and the reasons therefor; the form of constituting a Grand Lodge *pro tempore*, as a precedent; and a full detail of the particulars, from the initiation of the movement until its final consummation in electing a Grand Master and closing the meeting.

There was a motive for the reticence of Anderson in not publishing the details to which we have referred, so necessary to form a correct judgment as to the legality or illegality, propriety or impropriety, right or wrong of the so-called revival. But Anderson was not alone interested in omitting to notice all of the important particulars of that revolutionary movement. All those engaged in the formation of the new Grand Lodge had particular reasons for not having their motives and intentions known to the public. It will be our province, in the course of our writing, to lay before our readers the motives that actuated the craft in London in organizing the new Grand Lodge, and the particular reasons for keeping from the public eye the information necessary to a proper understanding of the cause or causes that influenced them to revolution.

It must be borne in mind, that, before Anderson's Constitutions, published in 1723, no publication on the subject of Masonry had been printed. Anderson says, 1720, page 613, ed. 1738, Hyneman's Reprint, "(for they had nothing yet in print,)" referring to some manuscripts "burnt by some scrupulous Brothers."

We maintain that prior to the revolution, 1717, the craft in the south of England still held their relation to the York Grand Lodge—that they were not independent of its authority—that there were Lodges in London and other parts of the south of England which did not join the revolutionists, but retained their connection with the Grand Lodge at York— that the revolution was without justification — that the assumed cause of Grand Master Wren neglecting the Lodges was simply an excuse to justify the ambitious Masons of London to carry into effect a long pre-entertained purpose—that the opportunity was favorable to their design, and hence the ignoring the existence of the York Grand Lodge and their silence in regard to everything concerning the revolutionary movement.

As we have already remarked, the 1723 Anderson publication does not mention the existence of the new Grand Lodge, only in the last paragraph, which closes with the name of the fifth Grand Master, the " Duke of Montague." This history is a curiosity in its way, and evidently designed to divert the attention away from the objective subject which such a publication ought to contain. For the benefit of our readers, we copy the commencement of the first three paragraphs. *First.* "Adam, our first parent, created after the image of God, the great Architect of the

Universe, must have had the liberal sciences, particu
larly geometry, written on his heart." *Second.* "No
doubt, Adam taught his sons geometry." *Third.*
"Nor can we suppose that Seth was less instructed,
who, being the prince of the other half of mankind,
and also the prime cultivator of astronomy, would
take equal care to teach geometry and *Masonry* to
his offspring."

The 1738 history, more elaborate, differs from the
preceding one, but is written in the same chimerical,
visionary, fanciful style, and notices all the Grand
Masters from Adam down to Caernarvon, 1738, but
omits to mention the Grand Lodge at York, or its
Grand Masters; only at page 592, (Vol. 2, Hyneman's
"Masonic Library,") in noticing the mythical attempt
of Queen Elizabeth to break up the annual meeting
of the York Grand Lodge, December 27th, 1561, and
noticing that "Francis Russel, Earl of Bedford, was
chosen Grand Master in the North," that is, in 1567.
There is one other place where Anderson mentions
"the old Lodge at York City," p. 676, to which we
will refer hereafter. The existence of the Grand
Lodge at York in 1567 is mentioned by Anderson;
also the charter purchased by Prince Edwin from his
brother, King Athelstan, and the meeting summoned
at York, 926, (page 580, Mas. Library;) and although
in the Elizabethan affair he mentions the Grand
Lodge at York as above, page 592, yet on the same
page, in referring to a Grand Master being chosen,
he only states "in the North;" otherwise the York
Grand Lodge is altogether overlooked in the entire
publication.

The evident intention of the revolutionists was not only to ignore the existence of the Grand Lodge at York, but of any York Lodges being in that jurisdiction. Their aim was through Anderson's publications to give prominence to their own organization, the new Grand Lodge, and to make it appear that there were no other Lodges of Masons in England in 1717, except the four concerned in the formation of the Grand Lodge. Anderson was well qualified for carrying out their views, not only as possessing the abilities, but his position in society — being a clergyman and being a revolutionist himself. He only wrote what he believed would be favorable to the new Grand Lodge and give it character; all else he omitted. He does not mention a single effort made by the London Masons to increase their privileges, nor the assuming powers existing in the Grand Lodge at York only; neither the encroachments upon its authority. He is silent on every subject in which the Grand Lodge at York would necessarily have to be mentioned. He writes for the revolutionists, and whilst he panders to their vanity, he caters for his own self-glorification.

The city of York, located in the northern part of England, did not offer inducements for enterprise, consequently the growth of population was limited, and therefore the fraternity made but slow progress in increasing their numbers; besides, the Masons there, as many of the old Masons since, and at the present day, were more intent in the conservation of Masonic principles and its esoteric teachings than an increase of membership, and therefore excluded themselves from the world's observation as much as possible. All pageantry and pompous exhibition at public parades and processions were considered by them as foreign to Masonic propriety, as well as the use of printer's ink for the purpose of bringing the fraternity prominently before the public. They eschewed notoriety, did not court the public gaze, made no outward demonstrations, did not decorate themselves with ornamental clothing, wore no gewgaws or trinkets in their daily life to attract the world's attention, and at their assemblings were sat- isfied with the plain unadorned white lambskin apron. The conditions of the London Masons were entirely different, and this caused them to view Freemasonry from a diverse standpoint to that of the York Masons. London increased vastly in population. It became a commercial centre. Enterprise sought it. Immigra- tion flowed there from every quarter, and every in- ducement existed for the encouragement of labor, trade, the arts, and enterprise of every description. This mixed and constantly increasing population eliminated different opinions and views on almost every subject, and it would have been strange if the craft had not been affected in some degree by the diverse opinions of differing nationalities on the sub- ject of Freemasonry.

If Anderson had been true to himself, and published to the world the facts as they occurred, and all the particulars of motives, objects, influences, &c., so that a correct judgment could have been formed by the craft, it would not only have been more satisfactory, but much that was done might have been overlooked, even the revolutionary act of establishing an independent Grand Lodge as a necessity growing out of the conditions as they existed.   But Anderson and those desiring independence did not deem it expedient to publish the facts to the world.   They are not only silent on every subject that would reveal their selfish and ambitious views and intentions, but they distort the existent facts by misrepresentation and false and deceptive statements, relying upon the characteristic reticence of the York Masons and the reputation of the author, Anderson, and the estimation in which the craft were held, that their version would not be controverted.   There is a meanness in the intended inferences to be drawn in Anderson's Constitutions discreditable to the Masonic institution, and disreputable to the author and all who sanctioned the publication.   The revolutionists in 1717 only consummated the object which the London Masons since the last half of the sixteenth century had in view, the throwing off their allegiance to the York Grand Lodge and establish an independent Masonic government. They had grown strong, Lodges and their membership had increased greatly; Masons from every country, coming to the metropolis on business or pleasure, visited their Lodges, and thus the London fraternity became widely known, and their acquaintance sought, which added greatly to their self-importance.   They adopted every means to bring themselves into notoriety, to render Masonry popular, and at every opportunity manifested a disposition by encroachments

and assumptive efforts to be a controlling power —
an independent sovereignty. They assumed that the
Light of Masonry only shone in their metropolis,
that its rays radiated from that centre, and that the
privilege to exercise the rights and franchises of Masonry was solely vested in the London craft, in the
Grand Lodge they had instituted.

Institutions and associative organizations are of
gradual growth. Far back in the ages the germinal
elements are being formed. They have neither shape
nor vitality in form. The elements aggregate as
thought is eliminated, and in the centuries they assume some form, — crude, immature, disconnected, it
is true, yet suited to the time and to the intelligence of
the period. On a sudden, a living thought is elicited,
as if by inspiration, from the interior perceptive faculties — the intellect is illumined, and a spark from
the brain, addressed in language adapted to the popular
ular sense, is accepted. A peaceful revolution or of
violence may result, angry words from hasty indi-
viduals of differing opinions may inflame unduly ex-
cited minds, whilst the crude form of aggregating
and aggregated elements is assuming a more perfect
shape, and the germ in embryo is being formed.

Thus institutions founded on beliefs, organized associations of every kind, governments, and the social
systems of the world, have been formed. It is a use-
less waste of time to seek the origin, the primal
thoughts of any institution or organized association
whatever. In regard to Freemasonry we know that
it existed prior to 1567. In that year we have the

earliest (so far as we now know) manifestation of a movement by the London Masons to assume, or aspire to self-government by encroaching upon the rightful authority of the York Grand Lodge. Until 1567, and subsequent, the supreme authority of the Grand Lodge at York was universally recognized by the craft, and, as Preston remarks, who was a member of one of the four London lodges which set up an in- dependent government in 1717, " To be ranked as de- scendants of the original York Masons was the glory and boast of the brethren in almost every country where Masonry has been regularly established, and from the prevalence and universality of the idea that in the city of York Masonry was first authorized by charter, the Masons of England have received tribute from the first states in Europe." This "Grand Lodge was held in the highest veneration, and every Mason in the kingdom considered himself bound by the charges which originally sprung from that body."

In consequence of certain *demands* of the London Masons in 1567, a Grand Master was appointed for the *South* of England. Preston, in referring to this appointment, says : "Sir Thomas Sackville held the office of Grand Master from 1561 to 1567, when he *resigned* (Anderson says, Accordingly, when Grand Master Sackville *demitted*, A. D. 1567) in favor of Fran- cis Russel, Earl of Bedford, and Sir Thomas Gresham, an eminent merchant, distinguished for his abilities and great success in trade. To the former the care of the brethren in the northern part of the kingdom was assigned, while the latter was *appointed to super-*

intend the meetings in the South, where the Society
had considerably increased, in consequence of the
honorable report which had been made to the Queen.
Notwithstanding this new appointment of a Grand
Master for the South, *the General Assembly continued
to meet in the city of York, as heretofore, where all the
records were kept; and to this Assembly appeals were
made on every important occasion.* We call special attention to this last clause, as we will have to refer to
it again, particularly the portion we have italicized.

We have no means of knowing what the character
of the demands were which impelled the York Grand
Lodge to appoint a Grand Master for the South of
England. They must have been of a grave nature to
cause the Grand Lodge to comply in a matter of such
moment affecting its rights and prerogatives. The necessity for such an appointment may well be questioned. There can be no doubt that the demands involved either a compliance or a rebellion against its authority. It was a seditious movement, a revolutionary design. In reference to this movement, Preston
wrote as follows: "As the constitutions of the English Lodges are derived from this General Assembly
at York — as all Masons are bound to observe and
preserve those in all time coming — and as there is
no satisfactory proof that such assembly was ever
regularly removed by the resolution of its members,
but that, on the contrary, the fraternity *still continue
to meet in that city* under this appellation, it may remain a doubt whether, while those constitutions exist
as the standard of Masonic conduct, that Assembly

may not justly claim the allegiance to which their original authority entitled them ; and whether any other convention of Masons, however great their consequence may be, can, consistently with those constitutions, withdraw their allegiance from that Assembly, or set aside an authority to which not only *antiquity*, but the *concurrent approbation of Masons for ages, under the most solemn engagements, have repeatedly given a sanction.*

"It is to be regretted that the idea of superiority, and a wish to acquire *absolute dominion*, should occasion a contest among Masons. Were the principles of the Order better understood, and more generally practised, the intention of the institution would be more fully answered. Every Mason would consider his brother as his fellow, and he who, by generous and virtuous actions, could best promote the happiness of society, would always be most likely to receive homage and respect."

These two paragraphs Oliver has altogether omitted in his reprint of Preston's "Illustrations of Masonry." We have no words to characterize the conduct of a man of his learning, of his position in society as a clergyman, his relations to the Masonic fraternity, and enjoying the world's esteem as an honorable and truthful man, in deceiving the public by omitting in his reprint work, believed to be a verbatim copy, such portions which he knew would be to the detriment of his Grand Lodge and damaging to the character of his antecedent laborers in the vineyard, Reverend Bros. Anderson, Desaguliers, &c. It was as reprehensible as it was dishonorable.

We commend the above-quoted paragraphs to the fraternity at the present time for the truly Masonic sentiments expressed in them, and for the clear allusions of the author in behalf of Truth to the rebellious spirit of the London Masons in forcing the York Grand Lodge to the alternative of either a renunciation of its authority and the establishment of a separate Masonic government, or a compliance with their unrighteous demands. The Grand Lodge chose the latter for the sake of unity and harmony among the craft. The York Masons were a long-suffering fraternity, and for the sake of peace and the honor and reputation of Masonry for many subsequent years, were obliged to submit to infractions of their rights by the London Masons, who, having gained the appointment of a Grand Master, continued from time to time to make encroachments and usurp privileges without saying "*by your leave, sir.*"

It must not be overlooked, as it is important to remember, that, notwithstanding the appointment of a Grand Master for the South of England, that the Grand Lodge at York was acknowledged as the legal and supreme head of the institution, to which body the whole fraternity owed allegiance. And in connection with the subject we quote again from Preston, who was a member of the London Grand Lodge, and without departing from the truth or ignoring it altogether, as Anderson and Oliver have, he was somewhat cautious in his remarks. He says: " There is every reason to believe that York was deemed the original seat of Masonic government in this country;

as no other place has pretended to claim it, and as the whole fraternity have, at various times, universally acknowledged allegiance to the authority established there; but whether the present association in that city be entitled to that allegiance is a subject of inquiry which it is not my province to investigate. To that Assembly recourse must be had for information. Thus much, however, is certain, that if a General Assembly or Grand Lodge was held there (of which there is little doubt, if we can rely on our records and constitution, as it is said to have existed there in Queen Elizabeth's time), there is no evidence of its regular removal to any other place in the kingdom : and upon that ground the brethren at York may probably claim the privilege of associating in that character. A number of respectable meetings of the fraternity appear to have been convened at sundry times in different parts of England; but we cannot find an instance on record, till a very late period, of a *general* meeting (so called) being held in any other place beside York."

There is a blank in the history of Masonry from 1567 to 1603, excepting the statement of Anderson, that after Thomas Gresham " Charles Howard, Lord of Effingham, was Grand Master in the South till 1588, then George Hastings, Earl of Huntington, till the Queen died unmarried on 24 March, 1602–3."

From the year 1567, when a Grand Master was appointed for the South, the Grand Lodge at York is not mentioned by Anderson or Preston until after the Revolution of 1717. It is entirely ignored, as if no

such body of Masons had ever existed. There may
have been such a case in the history of humanity as
children so devoid of affection and all moral sense as
to obliterate all evidence of their parents' existence,
or having existed, and effacing every trace by changing their own names and denying their paternity as
well as their birthplace; if so, it furnishes a parallel
to the conduct of the London Masons for two centuries from the time of the appointment of Grand Master Gresham. And in strict conformity with their
rebellious attempt at that time, in having secured the
appointment which apparently satisfied them for a
brief period only, as it appears from no mention being
made that the Grand Lodge at York was not con-
sulted, and had no voice in the selection of the two
mentioned successors to Grand Master Gresham.

The successor to Hastings was the celebrated Inigo
Jones, who was under King James I. in 1603 chosen
with the title "Grand Master of England," which
title was continued to subsequent Grand Masters in
the South. He, Inigo Jones, held Quarterly Communications of the Grand Lodge and the Annual
General Assembly, and was annually re-chosen till
1618.

Here we find, in addition to the assumption of a
prerogative pertaining solely to the York Grand
Lodge, the London Masons usurping a title intended
to convey the belief that no other Grand Lodge
existed in England, which was a most wicked and
malicious deception, a vile, dishonorable, and contemp-
tibly mean resort to further their selfish, ambitious

designs.   The intention of assuming the title of Grand
Master of England was to weaken the York Grand
Lodge, and by continued efforts to drive it out of existence, to absorb its membership, and thus possess
complete supremacy throughout the whole of England.   And in accord with the assumptions and designs of the London Masons, the Grand Master, Inigo
Jones, commenced holding quarterly communications,
the annual General Assembly, and constituting Lodges,
which were all usurpations of prerogatives belonging
solely and exclusively to their parent body, the Grand
Lodge at York.   We refer the reader to the preceding extracts from Preston as confirmatory of our
statements in regard to the General Assembly being
held at York, and on which subject Anderson is silent
and purposely so in his omissions to notice the York
Grand Lodge.

William, Earl of Pembroke, succeeded Inigo Jones
as Grand Master, and continued in office until 1630,
when he *demitted*, as Anderson has it, and was succeeded by Henry Danvers, Earl of Danby, — Preston says, *resigned* in favor of Henry Danvers, Earl of
Danby, who in 1633 was succeeded by Thomas Howard, Earl of Arundel, who in 1635 was succeeded by
Francis Russel, Earl of Bedford.   In 1636 Inigo
Jones was again chosen Grand Master, and continued
in office, as Preston says, "till his death in 1646."
Anderson says: "Inigo Jones, aged 80 years, died
at London, and was buried in St. Bennet's Church
at Paul's wharf on 26 June, 1652."   With the discrepancy of dates we have no concern.   It may be

that the body lay in state from 46 to 52, or was rein-
terred in the latter year, as Anderson does not mention when he died, or one or the other is in error.
Both Preston and Anderson are silent on the subject
of Masonry from the decease of Inigo Jones until
1663, except the following remarks by Preston: "The
breaking out of the civil wars obstructed the progress
of Masonry in England for some time; but after the
Restoration, it began to revive under the patronage
of Charles II., who had been received into the Order
during his exile."

On the 27th of December, 1663, a General Assembly was held, at which Henry Jermyn, Earl of St.
Albans, was chosen Grand Master, who appointed Sir
John Denham his Deputy, and Sir CHRISTOPHER WREN
and John Webb, Grand Wardens. At this General
Assembly, six Regulations were made in keeping with
the sentiments we have expressed to abnegate the
existence of their mother Grand Lodge, the Grand
Lodge at York. The *first* of these Regulations is as
follows: "That no person, of what degree soever,
be made or accepted a Freemason unless in a regular
Lodge, whereof one to be a Master or a Warden in
that limit or division where such Lodge is kept, and
another to be a Craftsman in the trade of Freemasonry." Here we have the first mention of a *regular* Lodge and associated with Master and Warden.
The *second :* "That no person hereafter shall be accepted a Freemason, but such as are of able body,
honest parentage, good reputation, and an observer
of the laws of the land." The *third* refers to "A

Certificate of the time and place, to be brought of those accepted a Freemason from the Lodge that accepted him, unto the Master who shall enroll the same, and give an account of all such acceptances at every General Assembly." The *fourth :* "That every person who is now a Freemason, shall bring to the Master a note of the time of his acceptation, to the end the same may be enrolled in such priority of place as the Brother deserves ; and that the company and fellows may the better know each other." The *fifth :* "That for the future the said fraternity of Free-masons shall be regulated and governed by *one Grand Master,* and as many Wardens as the said society shall think fit to appoint at every General Assembly." The *sixth :* " That no person shall be accepted unless he be twenty-one years old or more."

The drift of these regulations can readily be understood, as well as their object and intent. The fifth regulation tells the whole story. *The said fraternity of Freemasons shall be regulated and governed by one Grand Master.* There never was more than one Grand Master at one time in the South of England, from the time of the intended revolt in 1567; and as he held the title of Grand Master of England, the regulation must have intended " one Grand Master " for the whole of England. The scope of these regulations was to *nonsuit,* to use a legal phrase, the York Masons. They could have no other object than the non-recognition of those not under their jurisdiction, of which the " certificate " was the evidence and the " note of acceptation."

Thomas Savage, Earl of Rivers, succeeded St. Albans as Master, June 24th, 1666, who appointed Christopher Wren his Deputy. On the 2d of September occurred the great fire in London, in the rebuilding of which Wren had such a prominent part. Anderson says, "After Grand Master Rivers *demitted*, 1674, George Villars, Duke of Bucks, succeeded as Grand Master of England." Preston wrote: " In 1674 the Earl of Rivers *resigned*, and was succeeded by George Villiers, Duke of Buckingham." Does Anderson use the word demitted for resigned? Anderson again writes, the Duke demitted 1679, and Preston says, *resigned* in favor of Henry Bennet, Earl of Arlington. The Earl of Arlington died in 1685, when "the Lodges met and elected Sir Christopher Wren Grand Master, who had been continued Deputy Grand Master from his first appointment in 1666." Sir Christopher Wren appears to have been the active mind of the fraternity from his first appointment, as he was useful in civil life after the great calamity, as the prince of architects of the time. He was fifty-three years of age when elected Grand Master. Anderson writes that " He annually met those brethren who could attend him, to keep up good usages, *till the Revolution.*" During this period, Anderson says: " Particular Lodges were not so frequent, and mostly occasional in the South, except in or near the places where great works were carried on. Thus, Sir Robert Clayton got an occasional Lodge," at Southwark, "near which a stated Lodge continued long afterwards. Besides that, and the old Lodge of St. Paul's, there

was another at Piccadilly, one near Westminster
Abbey, another near Covent Garden, one in Holborn,
one on Tower Hill, and *some more* that assembled
statedly."

In 1695, Charles Lennox, Duke of Richmond and
Lennox, was chosen Grand Master. "Sir Christopher
Wren was his Deputy Grand Master, who acted as
before at the head of the craft, and was again chosen
Grand Master, A. D. 1698." We have been quoting
Anderson. Preston says, "Grand Master Wren con-
tinued at the head of the fraternity till the death of
the King, 1702." Anderson, writing of 1707, says:
"Yet still in the South the Lodges were more and
more disused, partly by the neglect of the Masters and
Wardens, and partly by not having a Noble Grand
Master *at London*, and the annual Assembly was not
duly attended." Here we have a hint reflecting upon
the want of attention to the craft by Sir Christopher
Wren, who certainly had few peers in that age. In
1708, Anderson still calls him Grand Master Wren,
when he erected the cross on the top of the cupola
of St. Paul's. And in the next paragraph Anderson
continues: "Some few years after this, Sir Christopher Wren neglected the office of Grand Master, yet
the old Lodge near St. Paul's and a few more continued their stated meetings till Queen Anne died,
1714." Now we come to the Revolution consummated by the London Masons in 1717, which Anderson, 1738 Const., inaugurates as follows:

"King George I. entered London most magnifi-
cently on 20th Sept., 1714, and after the rebellion

was over, A. D. 1716, the few Lodges at London, finding themselves *neglected* by Sir Christopher Wren, thought fit to cement under a Grand Master as the center of union and harmony, viz., the Lodges that met

"1. At the Goose and Gridiron Ale-house, in St. Paul's Churchyard;

"2. At the Crown Ale-house, in Parker's Lane, near Drury-Lane;

"3. At the Apple-Tree Tavern, in Charles Street, Covent Garden;

"4. At the Rummer and Grapes Tavern, in Channel Row, Westminster.

" They and *some old Brothers* met at the said Apple-Tree, and having put into the chair the oldest Master Mason (now the Master of a Lodge), they constituted themselves a Grand Lodge *pro tempore* in due form, and forthwith revived the Quarterly Communication of the officers of Lodges (called the Grand Lodge), resolved to hold the Annual Assembly and Feast, and then to choose a Grand Master from among themselves till they should have the honor of a Noble Brother at their head.

"Accordingly, on St. John Baptist's day, in the third year of King George I., A. D. 1717, the Assembly and Feast of the *Free and Accepted Masons* was held at the foresaid Goose and Gridiron Ale-house. Before dinner, the oldest Master Mason (now the Master of a Lodge) in the chair, proposed a list of proper candidates; and the brethren by a majority of hands elected Mr. Antony Sayer, gentleman, Grand Master

of Masons, who being forthwith invested with the
badges of office and power by the said oldest Master,
and installed, was duly congratulated by the Assembly who paid him the homage."

We make the following comments on the above
narration of Anderson, whose Book of Constitutions
was authorized to be published by order of the London
Grand Lodge in 1738.   After having been submitted
to a committee of the Grand Officers, and having it
three years under consideration, its publication was
ordered, with the approbation of the Grand Officers
printed in it, "as the only Book of Constitutions for
the use of the Lodges of the Free and Accepted Masons, &c."   Taking fully into consideration the state
of society in the early part of the last century, the
reader can have no high opinion of London Freemasonry at the period referred to, nor of the moral
status of the craft, according to the places at which
the four Lodges held their meetings, and the place.
where the Grand Master was chosen and installed.
These were fitting places to concoct and consummate
revolution by persons congregating at such haunts.
But the questions arise, 1st, Were there only four
Lodges in London at that time? 2d, By what authority were these Lodges constituted? 3d, Who were
those "some old Brothers"?   4th, And how many of
them?   5th, Did Masonry indeed decline in consequence of being neglected by Grand Master Wren?

The first four questions we will hereafter consider.
In regard to the fifth we observe that in 1707 Anderson says: "In the South the Lodges were more and

more disused, partly by *the neglect of the Masters and Wardens*, and partly by *not having a Noble Grand Master* at London." The intimation here is very plain that it was in consequence of the lukewarmness of the Masters and Wardens that Lodges declined, or " disused," as Anderson has it, the cause for which we will hereafter revert to. The not having a *Noble Grand Master* had nothing to do with the decline of Lodges or want of interest on the part of the Masters and Wardens. A Royal Grand Master could not compel the Masters and Wardens to attend their Lodges if they felt no interest in the institution. Sir Christopher Wren was Grand Master at that time, 1707, was a member of Parliament, and represented several boroughs, active and in full vigor of his powers. Neither the attendance at Lodges nor any proper interest in Masonry, depends upon a Grand Master. In this age of concentrated powers in Grand Lodges and Grand Masters, no particular interest is infused into the Institution through them. The subordinate Lodges alone possess the vital power to keep the institution alive, and without Grand Masters and Grand Lodges Masonry would flourish as well as with them, and perhaps retain more of its cosmopolitan character than at the present.

The inference attached to G. M. Wren of neglect is most malicious. Did the Masters and Wardens need the promptings of the Grand Master to urge them to discharge their Masonic duties? If they were indifferent to the affairs of Masonry, to their obligations, and had no inclination to attend Lodge meetings, the Grand Master could not be censurable therefor; and if they did need his promptings to influence them to discharge their duties, they were worse than dead Masons, and in their pretentious connection with the fraternity bringing dishonor and disgrace upon the institution. When Lodges die out because of non-attendance of the members at their meetings for lack of interest in Masonry, the conclusion must be the material of such Lodges must have been too imperfect originally to be worked into the Masonic temple. Of such material mainly seems to have been the London craft for two centuries from the appointment of the first Grand Master, in 1567.

Grand Master Wren died in 1723, aged ninety-one years. He was in active public life till 1713 at least. The purity of his life was never tarnished, and with the exception of Anderson, no reflection was ever cast upon his fair fame. But it is preposterous to suppose that the prosperity of the Masonic institution or its success depended exclusively on a single individual, however exalted, intelligent, or indefatigable in his attentions. Anderson would have us believe that because G. M. Wren, after having passed his threescore and ten years, neglected the craft, and in consequence the Lodges died out; but it appears he was *continued* Grand Master up to the revolution, 1717, and yet the Lodges had it in their power at any time to choose another Grand Master if Sir Christopher had indeed neglected the fraternity. Under any aspect of the case, the conclusion must be arrived at, the fault must have been in the material of which the London craft was composed.

The history of the London Masons, which we have only briefly noticed, we have extracted mainly from Anderson's Constitutions, 1738 ed. But as he was one of the revolutionists, and an active promoter of the revolution, and a participator in the formation of the new Grand Lodge in London, his historical statements must be taken with all due allowances, to present as plausible an account as possible favorable to the revolution, the apparent necessity for the movement, and the omitting of any allusions to the existence of other Masonic bodies in England, by impressing his readers with the belief that none such did exist. And as Anderson does not mention any difficulties among the craft, or contrariety of opinions etween them, the natural deduction is, that unity, armony, and brotherly love prevailed, and that a 'ted fraternity existed throughout England.

We have for many years entertained the belief that Anderson was not truthful, that the rose-colored view of the conditions as stated by him was fictitious, that he did not state matters as they really existed, and that if in his manuscript he had mentioned or only alluded to the existence of Lodges holding under the York Grand Lodge, or differences of opinions and feelings of opposition among the members of the "four (London) Lodges" and those "old Brothers," the Grand Officers and the Grand Lodge would have caused a line to be drawn over the writing, as being detrimental to the new organization. But Anderson understood the position too well to commit to writing aught that might even seemingly be prejudicial to the revolutionary movement, or that might be so considered by posterity.

As to our question, " Were there only four Lodges in London at that time?" at the revolution in 1717. Admitting only for a moment the statement of Anderson to be true, London did not embrace the whole of the South of England; and as many Lodges had been constituted in the South during the prior one hundred and fifty years, why did not a single one participate in the revolution? Had they no information of the contemplated movement? Had they no notice of the contemplated formation of a Grand Lodge? There is no mention of any other Lodges being represented than the four London Lodges. The revolutionary movement seems to have been a *coup d'état* movement, suddenly sprung upon the craft by Anderson, Desaguliers, Payne, and some of the leading Masons in London. That there were other Lodges in London and other parts of the South of England there can be no doubt ; and even some holding under the York Grand Lodge. The silence of Anderson in regard to York Masons may satisfy some, who " swear by him," that that body did not exist. We will see hereafter.

In addition to " some old Brothers " who met with the four Lodges at the Apple-Tree Tavern, Anderson mentions on the next page, " Now several old Brothers that had neglected the craft visited the Lodges." Those *old Brothers* visiting the Lodges to our view has a suspicious look. The meagre statement, with-out names, or how many of them, or from whence they hailed, seems to give an imaginary aspect to the two statements, or the statements, if true, would imply that there were many of such brothers, and, consequently, Lodges in which they were made; and it is possible, too, that those old brothers were prompted more by curiosity than anything else. But that there were Masons in London at the time of the revolution who did not assent to the formation of the new Grand Lodge, and also some York Masons who would not participate, there can be little doubt.

Wm. Sandys, F. A. S., P. M. Grand Master's Lodge, wrote a work, published in London in 1829, by Crew & Spencer, entitled, "A Short View of the History of Freemasons," dedicated to the Grand Lodge, in which he mentions that "in the beginning of the reign of George the First, an unfortunate *schism* arose in the Society in consequence of Sir Christopher Wren — who was then about ninety years of age and unable to attend to any active duties of the craft — having been superseded in his office of Surveyor of Buildings to the King by Mr. William Benson, under whose direction the *generality of Master Masons in London refused to meet; and the country Lodges, especially at York and in Scotland, kept inviolate the Ancient Landmarks, &c., of the Order."* (See Hyneman's Masonic Library, vol. i. p. 739.) The above extract from the intelligent author is clearly to the point in his reference to a schism among the craft, and corroborates our statement that there were other Lodges and Masons in London that had no part in the formation of the new Grand Lodge, and both Anderson and Preston imply as much.

Preliminary to a continuation of the subject, we will briefly state right here our views of the real cause of the difficulties, the reference to illegal assemblies of Masons in subsequent years, of Lodges not meeting, of the erasure of Lodges, of all the statements of irregularities among the craft, of inferred infringements, in fact, of all and everything that gave seeming offence or rather annoyance to the London Grand Lodge referred to by Anderson, Entick, Blaney, and Preston, the latter mainly echoing the statements of the former in the interest of his own Lodge, which was one of the four Lodges which formed the London Grand Lodge.

The real cause was, that there were *Lodges and Masons in London holding their allegiance to the York Grand Lodge that would not countenance nor acknowledge the new London Grand Lodge. There was no actual schism in* 1738, *as Anderson, Preston, and recent writers assume.* The object of the revolutionary body was to stigmatize those who would not come under its authority, and such as had left it for its innovating tendencies and preferred their connection with the original Masonic body, the York Grand Lodge. *It was the successors of these who, in* 1813, *formed the union with the London Grand Lodge.* There was no third Grand Lodge formed in England out of those Lodges which for good and sufficient reasons remained true to their allegiance to the York Grand Lodge, nor of those who left the London Grand Lodge. *The story of a third Grand Lodge is wholly mythical.* The object in making it appear that the Lodges which severed their connection with the London Grand Lodge had formed themselves into a Grand Lodge, was to be consistent with the original design of the London Masons, to keep out of view altogether the York Grand Lodge, to suppress all information of such a Masonic Body being in existence. We now return again to Anderson, and in our future remarks will corroborate the above.

The title given to Mr. Antony Sayer, Gentleman, chosen Grand Master in 1717, was " GRAND MASTER OF MASONS," not, as heretofore, " of England," and this title was continued to subsequent Grand Masters down to near the union, 1813. The assumption of that title, in contradistinction to the title of prior Grand Masters, will be obvious as in keeping with their un-Masonic designs. The election of that Gentleman " by a majority of hands," is sufficiently significant. Why elect by a show of hands? is a pertinent inquiry. It was not unanimous. What was the majority? and who were the other candidates? G. M. Sayer issued a summons in which he " *commanded* the Masters and Wardens of Lodges to meet the Grand Officers every Quarter in Communication." The issuing of an imperative summons does not speak well for the fidelity of the craft who inaugurated the revolution. The second Grand Master of Masons, George Payne, Esq., 1718, " recommended the strict observance of the Quarterly Communication," which was a milder course. But as showing that the fraternity were not well versed in the ancient usages of Masonry, he " desired any Brethren **to**

bring to the Grand Lodge any old writings and records concerning Masons and Masonry, in order to
shew the usages of antient times." We can well
smile at the observations of Lawrence Dermott in
his Ahiman Rezon on the subject of the kind of
Masonry worked by these early revolutioners.

John Theophilus Desaguliers, LL.D. and F.R.S.,
was the third Grand Master. He "revived the old
regular and peculiar Toasts or Healths of the Free
Masons." The Rev. Dr. Desaguliers, like his Rev.
Bro. Anderson, must have been fond of the socialities
of the festive board, and may have originated the
ceremonies observed at what is called the Table
Lodge. No doubt John and James, the two boon-
companions, were regular attendants at such Lodge
occasions, and one or the other inspired, as it were,
called forth from the soul-stirring influences of the
festivities at the "feast," on the occasion of Bro. Desaguliers' installation as Grand Master, the peculiar
toasts or healths of the Freemasons. And here we
have again "several *old* Brothers that had neglected the
Craft, visited the Lodges." Anderson does not say
where they hailed from, what Lodge, how many. They
were visitors, and had neglected the craft, and adds,
"Some Noblemen were *also* made Brothers." What
are we to understand by the word "also"? Was it
to give the reader to understand that these "old
Brothers" had affiliated with a Lodge under their
jurisdiction? Why use the word at all? And Anderson remarks: "Now several old Brothers, that had
neglected the Craft, visited the Lodges; some Noble-

men were also made Brothers, and more new Lodges
were constituted."

" George Payne, Esq., again Grand Master of Masons, 1720, was the fourth in succession." Anderson reports that this year some " very valuable manuscripts (for they had nothing yet in print), concerning
the fraternity, were burned by some scrupulous
Brothers, that those papers might not fall into strange
hands."

John, Duke of Montagu, 1721, was the fifth G. M.
He " and the Lodge finding fault with all the copies
of the *old Gothic Constitutions*, ordered, September 29,
1721, Brother James Anderson, A. M., to *digest the
same in a new and better method*." Fourteen learned
Brothers were appointed, Dec. 27, to examine the
manuscript and to make report. On March 25th,
1722, the " Committee of fourteen reported they had
perused the manuscript, viz., The History, Charges,
Regulations and Master's Song, and after some
amendments had approved of it; upon which the
Lodge desired the G. M. to order it to be printed."
" Grand Master Montagu's good government inclined
the *better sort* to continue him in the Chair another
year; and therefore they delayed to prepare the
feast." " But Philip, Duke of Wharton, lately made
a Brother, tho' not the Master of a Lodge, being ambitious of the Chair, got a number of others to meet
him at Stationers' Hall, 24 June, 1722, and having no
Grand Officers, they put in the chair the oldest Master Mason, (who was not the *present* Master of a
Lodge, also irregular,) and without the usual decent

ceremonials, the said old Mason proclaimed aloud, 'Philip Wharton, Duke of Wharton, Grand Master of Masons!' Therefore the noble Brothers and all those that would not countenance irregularities, disowned Wharton's authority, till worthy Brother Montagu healed the breach of harmony, by summoning the Grand Lodge to meet, 17 January, 1723, when the Duke of Wharton, promising to be true and faithful, D. G. M. Beal proclaimed Philip Wharton, Duke of Wharton, Grand Master of Masons."

At this meeting, "Anderson produced the *new* Book of Constitutions, now in print, which was again approved, with the addition of the *antient manner*(?) *of constituting a Lodge.*" The Wharton episode is briefly stated by Anderson as we have written it, but that there was trouble "in the camp," and much untold more than was printed, there can be no doubt. We pass over the successions of Grand Masters contained in Anderson's 1738 Constitutions, also the Proceedings had in Grand Lodge, as *the whole work is reprinted in Second Volume of our Masonic Library*, pp. 527–693. We will only notice the authority for publication. Grand Lodge, 24 February, 1735. "Brother Anderson, Author of the Book of Constitutions, representing that a new edition was become necessary, and that he had prepared materials for it, the Grand Master and the Lodge ordered him to lay the same before the present and former Grand Officers, that they may report their opinion to the Grand Lodge." Grand Lodge, January 25, 1738, "approved of this New Book of Constitutions, and ordered the author, Brother Anderson, to print the same with the addition of the new Regulation IX."

Preston, immediately following the choice of John, Duke of Montagu, as Grand Master of Masons, has the following extended notice of the York Grand Lodge:

"While Masonry was spreading its influence over the Southern part of the kingdom, it was not neglected in the North. The General Assembly, or Grand Lodge at York, continued to meet regularly as heretofore. In 1705, under the direction of Sir George Tempest, bart., then Grand Master, several Lodges met, and many worthy brethren were initiated in York and its neighborhood. Sir George being succeeded by the Right Hon. Robert Benson, Lord Mayor of York, a number of meetings of the fraternity was held at different times in that city, and the grand feast during his Mastership is said to have been very brilliant. Sir William Robinson, bart., succeeded Mr. Benson in the office of Grand Master, and the fraternity seem to have considerably increased in the North under his auspices. He was succeeded by Sir Walter Hawkesworth, bart., who governed the Society with great credit. At the expiration of his Mastership, Sir George Tempest was elected a second time Grand Master; and from the time of his election in 1714 to 1725, the Grand Lodge continued regularly to assemble in York under the direction of Charles Fairfax, Esq., Sir Walter Hawkesworth, bart., Edward Bell, Esq., Charles Bathurst, Esq., Edward Thompson, Esq., M. P., John Johnson,

M. D., and John Marsden, Esq., all of whom, in rota-
tion, during the above period regularly filled the office
of Grand Master in the North of England."

[We believe that nothing can be more conclusive
than that the York Grand Lodge continued its existence after the revolution of the London Masons in
forming an independent Grand Lodge; and as it existed at the time of the revolution, 1717, the London
Masons had no excuse nor justification for their rebellion; and to charge the decline of the Lodges to
Sir Christopher Wren, and as justifying them in their
rebellion to the constitutional Masonic Grand Lodge,
was a contemptible and malicious evasion of the truth,
purposely intended to intimate that there was no governing Masonic body in England, that the York Grand
Lodge had ceased to exist, and therefore the necessity
of forming a Grand Lodge for themselves. The York
Grand Lodge in 1567 gave permission to the London
Masons to select a Grand Master for the South of
England, and there is no evidence that its consent
was not renewed on future occasions, when necessary,
in consequence of the Grand Master demitting, declining the office, or in case of death, until Sir Christopher Wren was chosen Grand Master, in 1698, and
who was continued in office until the London Masons
set up a Grand Lodge for themselves without the
consent of their mother Grand Lodge at York.]

"From this account, which is *authenticated by the
books of the Grand Lodge in York*, it appears that the
revival of Masonry in the South of England did not
interfere with the proceedings of the fraternity in the

North. For a series of years the most perfect har
mony subsisted between the two Grand Lodges, and
private Lodges flourished in both parts of the kingdom under their separate jurisdiction. The only distinction which the Grand Lodge in the North *appears
to have retained* after the revival of Masonry in the
South, is in the title which they claim, viz., THE
GRAND LODGE OF ALL ENGLAND; while the Grand
Lodge in the South passes only under the denomination of *The Grand Lodge of England.* The latter, on
account of its situation, being encouraged by some
of the principal nobility, soon acquired consequence
and reputation; while the former, restricted to fewer
though not less respectable members, seemed gradually to decline. Till within these few years, however,
the authority of the Grand Lodge in York has never
been CHALLENGED; on the contrary, every Mason in
the kingdom has always held it in the highest veneration, and considered himself bound by the charges
which originally sprung from that assembly. To be
ranked as descendants of the original York Masons
was the glory and boast of the brethren in almost
every country where Masonry has been regularly
established; and from the prevalence and universality
of the idea that in the city of York Masonry was first
authorized by charter, the Masons of England have
received tribute from the first states in Europe. It is
much to be regretted that any separate interests
should have destroyed the social intercourse of Masons; but it is no less remarkable than true, that the
brethren in the North and those in the South are now

in a manner unknown to each other. *Notwithstand-ing the pitch of eminence and splendor at which the Grand Lodge in London has arrived, neither the Lodges of Scotland nor Ireland court its correspondence.* This unfortunate circumstance has been attributed to *the introduction of a few modern innovations among the Lodges in the South.* To remove this prejudice, the Grand Lodge have resolved *to resume the original practices* of the society, and have instituted a Lodge of Promulgation for the more regular diffusion of the art. They have also established a friendly intercourse with the Grand Lodge of Scotland, which is now under the banner of His Royal Highness the Prince of Wales. As to the coolness which has subsisted between the Grand Lodge in York and the Grand Lodge in London, another reason is assigned. A few brethren at York having on some trivial occasion seceded from their ancient Lodge, they applied to London for a warrant of constitution; and without inquiry into the merits of the case, their application was honored. Instead of being recommended to the mother Lodge to be restored to favor, these brethren were encouraged in their revolt, and permitted, under the banner of the Grand Lodge in London, to open a new Lodge in the city of York itself. This unguarded act justly offended the Grand Lodge of York, and occasioned a breach which time and a proper attention to the rules of the Order only can repair."

Preston is the only authority that the York Grand Lodge ever claimed, much less "retained" the title of "The Grand Lodge of all England." All that

Preston has written in regard to the distinctive titles
of the York and London Grand Lodges is the mere
imagination of his own brain, to give interest to his
book. His "illustrations" can only be considered in
the light of being *illustrated* with fanciful conceptions
of his own mind, and intermixed with Anderson's
relations without regard to times or concurrent events.
As in regard to Anderson, so the fraternity have received the statements of Preston, which he originated
in other important matters as well as in the distinction of the titles of the two Grand Lodges as veritable truths; and these have not only been repeatedly
quoted, but many a theory has been founded upon
the imaginary creations of Preston, and outwrought
in histories and other works on Masonry. Why
Preston calls it the Grand Lodge in the North, and
why make a local distinction North and South, are
questions not easily answered. Neither Anderson nor
Entick make these distinctions in referring to the
Grand Lodges.

It is to be regretted that Preston mixes up events
more than threescore years apart in this otherwise
valuable reference to the York Grand Lodge. The
Lodge of Promulgation was appointed in 1809, a few
years prior to the union which took place in 1813.
The friendly intercourse with the Grand Lodge of
Scotland commenced in 1806, and the granting a warrant of constitution to seceders at York must have
been in 1738, when the Earl of Crawford was Grand
Master. If Preston had not been biassed or influenced
to write in the unsatisfactory manner he has, by the

London Grand Lodge, with the intent to confuse the reader, he would have given us the current events in the order in which they occurred. But the interest of the Grand Lodge had to be subserved, and that was more important to the London Masons than to be faithful to truth.

The interesting and important matter contained in the said extract needs no excuse for its length. It must, however, always be borne in mind that Preston was a member of the Lodge of Antiquity, and wrote chiefly in the interest of the London Grand Lodge, which will account for his use of terms modifying to an extent the intolerant, illiberal, un-Masonic acts of the London Grand Lodge, as the introduction of a "*few modern innovations* among the Lodges in the South," as if the Grand Lodge did not authorize those innovations; and simply "*a few modern*," as if of no material importance, when every intelligent and "booked up" Mason knows that some of these innovations embraced alterations and changes in the secret work, in contravention of Masonic obligations, as well as the mode of recognition and examination. The intent of these innovations was to prevent the York Masons from visiting their Lodges; but it was soon discovered that did not answer the purpose, as some of the London Masons fraternized with the York Masons, and some came under the York banner.

Again, "a *few* brethren *seceded* from their ancient Lodge," should have been, were *expelled*. But Preston has in the above extract given much for consid-

eration and reflection, and to a correct understanding,
so far as the circumstances permitted, of the active
existence of the York Grand Lodge in 1705 and onward, and the causes of coolness between it and the
London Grand Lodge, provoked by the latter by its
malicious, aggressive, un-Masonic invasion of the
rights and jurisdiction of their Mother Grand Lodge.
There are no words in any language that can properly express the flagrant enormity of the conduct of
the London Grand Lodge in a moral or Masonic point
of view, especially if we consider, that, notwithstanding the aggressive acts of the London Grand Lodge
for a century and a half prior, and its revolutionary
act in establishing an independent Grand Lodge, the
York Grand Lodge displayed a most Masonic and
fraternal policy in giving no umbrage and not noticing the grossly un-Masonic course pursued by the
London Masons.

In 1734, Earl Crawford Grand Master, Preston reports the following proceedings of the London Grand
Lodge. "A few resolutions also passed respecting
illegal conventions of Masons, at which it was reported
many persons had been initiated into Masonry on
small and unworthy considerations." Anderson does
not mention this, neither Entick, (1756 ed., Const.)
Preston no doubt copied from the Grand Lodge
Records. We have already stated that these so-called
"*illegal* conventions of Masons" by the London
craft, were *regular bodies of Masons holding under the
York Grand Lodge*, and were called illegal because
they would not affiliate with the London Grand

Lodge. The making Masons "on small and unworthy considerations" was an *addenda* made to give
color to the reports which were doubtless imaginary.

We now invite attention to the following paragraph which immediately follows the above brief extract, and which is neither in Anderson's nor Entick's
Books of Constitutions: "The Earl of Crawford seems
to have made another encroachment on the jurisdiction of the Grand Lodge in the City of York, by constituting two Lodges within their districts, and by
granting, without their consent, three deputations,
one for Lancashire, a second for Durham, and a third
for Northumberland. This circumstance the Grand
Lodge in York highly resented, and ever after seems
to have viewed the proceedings of the brethren in
the South with a jealous eye; as all friendly intercourse ceased, and the York Masons from that moment considered their interests distinct from the
Masons under the Grand Lodge in London." Preston has a note to this paragraph as follows:

"In confirmation of the above fact, I shall here in-
sert a paragraph copied from the Book of Constitutions published in 1738. After inserting a list of
Provincial Grand Masters appointed for different
places abroad, it is thus expressed: 'All these foreign Lodges are under the patronage of our Grand
Master of England; but the old Lodge at York city,
and the Lodges of Scotland, Ireland, France, and
Italy, *affecting independency*, are under their own
Grand Masters; though they have the same constitutions, charges, regulations, &c., for substance, with

their brethren of England, and are equally zealous for the Augustan stile, and the secrets of the ancient and honorable Fraternity.'" (Hyneman's Masonic Library, vol. ii., p. 676.)

In the whole course of our life we have never seen so great an outrage upon the common-sense of the reading world as the intent embraced in the last paragraph taken from Anderson's Constitutions, 1738 ed. The very essence of malice is contained in the two words we have italicized; they manifest in their designed sense the constituent principles that animated the London revolutionists. There could be no greater manifestation of the most intense malignity, of expression of seeming power, as if they alone possessed the sole authority of Masonic government on this little planet. The York Grand Lodge, the Mother of Masonry in England, *affecting independency !* because, and because only, it gave no formal recognition to the revolutionary body, would not acknowledge it as an independent Grand Lodge, or, as a legally constituted one; would not go contrary to its fair fame, its antecedent history, by giving even the faintest color of seeming recognition to an un-Masonic or illegal act. To force out of existence the York Grand Lodge by any and all possible, fair or unfair, means, was the object and aim of the London Masons. That body stood in the way of the London Masons, who aimed to possess entire control of Masonry in England. It must be remembered that Anderson's Constitutions, of which the above paragraph forms a part, was not only approved by the former and present Grand Officers, but also by the Grand Lodge at a Grand Communication, and its sanction given as printed in the Book. Therefore Anderson was not alone in the publication of that arrogant and malicious paragraph, but the whole of the Grand Officers and members of the Grand Lodge were responsible for the unprovoked, dishonorable, and untruthful statements. The only Grand Lodge assuming or *affecting independency* was the London Grand Lodge, which object the London Masons had in view all the years from 1567 down to the revolution 1717. But the arrogance of including *Scotland, Ireland, France,* and *Italy,* is of so insolent and impudent a character, that, if it were not of so serious a nature, we could smile at the bold effrontery in stating such audacious falsehoods.

On the 27th of April, 1738, the Marquis of Carnarvon was installed Grand Master of Masons. Preston observes that "two deputations for the office of Provincial Grand Master were granted by his lordship, one for the Caribbee Islands, and the other for the West Riding of Yorkshire. This latter appointment was considered as a third encroachment on the jurisdiction of the Grand Lodge in York, and so widened the original breach between the brethren in the North and the South of England, that from henceforward *all future correspondence between the Grand Lodges totally ceased."*

It is well to remember the closing remark made by Preston in this quotation: "From henceforward all future correspondence between the Grand Lodges totally ceased." This was in 1738. It would seem that prior to this invasion of the jurisdiction of the York Grand Lodge, there *was* a correspondence kept up between the two Grand Lodges, notwithstanding the prior encroachments of the London Masons and their violations of Masonic comity, of Masonic principles, and rights of jurisdiction. As all correspondence then totally ceased, it became very convenient afterwards for the London Masons, including Preston, to erase the word York from their vocabulary, and instead of Ancient York Masons, which was the proper title, although not mentioned in any of the books of the London Masons, they dropped the name York, and, as we will see further on, called those who seceded from them and afiliated with the York Lodges, "Ancient Masons," as well as the York Lodges, Lodges of Ancient Masons, or Ancients, the object of which will be revealed hereafter in making it appear that the Ancients formed a Grand Lodge. Hence we find the London Grand Lodge all through its future transactions animadverting against that body and stigmatizing it and its members as illegal, because they did not work under its Constitution. But it will be seen towards the close of this book, that the union was formed through the unbiassed intelligence of the Prince of Wales, Grand Patron of Masons with the " Free and Accepted Masons of England, according to the *old institutions*," who were the Ancient York Masons.

So far, we have followed Preston to the close of Anderson's Constitutions, 1738 edition, and purpose following Preston further on, as Entick's Book of

Constitutions is written in the same meagre and unsatisfactory evasive style of Anderson, and gives us
little information aside from successions of Grand
Masters and accompanying ceremonials.   We will,
however, have to recur to Anderson again and also
to Entick.

About the close of Carnarvon's term as Grand Master, Preston reports as follows: "Some disagreeable
altercations arose in the Society about this period.   A
number of dissatisfied brethren having separated themselves from the regular lodges, held meetings in different places for the purpose of initiating persons
into Masonry, contrary to the laws of the Grand
Lodge.   These seceding brethren taking advantage
of the breach which had been made in the friendly
intercourse between the Grand Lodges of London
and York, on being censured for their conduct, immediately *assumed* at their irregular meetings, without authority, the character of York Masons.   Measures were adopted to check them, which stopped their
progress for some time ; but taking advantage of the
*general murmur spread abroad on account of some inno-
vations that had been introduced,* and which *seemed to
authorize* an omission of, and a variation in the ancient ceremonies, they rose again into notice.   *This
imprudent measure of the regular lodges* offended
many old Masons, but through the mediation of John
Ward, Esq., afterwards lord viscount Dudley and
Ward, matters were accommodated, and the brethren
seemingly reconciled.   This, however, proved only a
temporary suspension of hostilities, for the flame

soon broke out again, and gave rise to commotions which afterwards materially interrupted the peace of the Society."

[The paragraph just quoted is evidence that perfect harmony did not exist among the craft under the London Grand Lodge. Preston cleverly makes it appear that it was the seceding London Masons who held meetings for the purpose of initiating persons contrary to the laws of their Grand Lodge, and who *assumed* the character of York Masons. The perversion of truth was in uniform accord with all the statements of the Masons under the London Grand Lodge in regard to the disaffected among their own members who affiliated with the York Lodges. Their whole aim and purpose was to ignore the existence of Ancient York Masons and Masonry, and to suppress by all possible means the fact that York Lodges were established, held meetings, and made Masons according to regular warrants of Constitution, or by legal and rightful authority. The efforts of Preston were in conformity with those of Anderson, and in appearance plausible, so that the superficial readers were easily deceived. The investigating mind, however, will remember Preston's own statements, copied from the Records, that the York Grand Lodge was an active body of Masons, and its Lodges and members in high repute. The *measures* adopted by the London Grand Lodge, "which stopped their progress for some time," and the "temporary suspension of hostilities," was well enough to state to give a color of relief as if the writer was unbiassed in

reference to the seceding members assuming the character of York Masons.   There was no need of *assuming*.   The York Masons had a better reputation, a
clearer and truer Masonic record, than the London
Masons, and therefore the members dissatisfied with
the conduct of the London Masons would naturally
go over and affiliate with the York Masons.]

"Lord Raymond succeeded the Marquis of Carnarvon in May, 1739, and under his Lordship's auspices
the Lodges were numerous and respectable.   Notwithstanding the flourishing state of the society, *irregularities continued to prevail*, and *several worthy brethren*,
still *adverse to the encroachments on the established system of the institution*, seemed to be highly disgusted
at the proceedings of the regular Lodges.   Complaints were preferred at every succeeding committee,
and the communications fully employed in adjusting
differences and reconciling animosities.   More secessions taking place, it became necessary to pass votes
of censure on the most refractory, and enact laws to
discourage irregular associations of the fraternity.
This brought the power of the Grand Lodge in question; and in opposition to the laws which had been
established in that assembly, Lodges were formed
without any legal warrant, and persons initiated into
Masonry for small and unworthy considerations.   To
disappoint the views of these deluded brethren, and
to distinguish the persons initiated by them, the Grand
Lodge *readily acquiesced in the imprudent measures
which the regular Masons had adopted* — measures
which even the urgency of the case could not war-

rant. Though this had the intended effect, it gave
rise to a new subterfuge. The brethren who had
seceded from the regular Lodges immediately an-
nounced independency, and assumed the appellation
of *ancient Masons*. They propagated an opinion that
the ancient tenets and practices of Masonry were
preserved by them, and that the regular Lodges, being composed of *modern* Masons, had adopted *new*
plans, and were not to be considered as acting under
the *old* establishment. To counteract the regulations
of the Grand Lodge, they instituted a *New Grand
Lodge in London*, professedly on the *ancient* system,
and contrary to their duty as Masons, under that assumed banner constituted several new Lodges in
opposition to the regular established authority. These
irregular proceedings they pretended to justify under
the *feigned* sanction of the *Ancient York* Constitution,
and many gentlemen of reputation being deceived by
this artifice, were introduced among them, so that
their Lodges daily increased. Without authority
from the Grand Lodge in York, or from any other
established power in Masonry, these refractory brethren persevered in the measures they had adopted,
formed committees, held communications, and even
appointed annual feasts. Under the false appellation
of the York banner, they gained the countenance of
the Scotch and Irish Masons, who, placing implicit
confidence in the representations made to them,
heartily joined in condemning the measures of the
regular Lodges in London, as tending in their opinion to introduce novelties into the society, and to

subvert the original plan of the institution. The
irregular Masons in London having thus acquired a
nominal establishment, noblemen of both kingdoms,
unacquainted with the origin of the separation, honored them with their patronage, and some respectable
names and Lodges were added to their list. [Of *late
years*, however, the fallacy has been fully detected by
the active diligence of a few zealous brethren, and
they have not been so successful : several of their best
members have deserted them, and many Lodges re-
nounced their banner, who have come under the patronage of the Grand Lodge of England. It is much
to be wished that a general union among all the Masons in the kingdom could be effected; and we are
now happy to hear that such a measure is likely soon
to be accomplished, through the mediation of a noble
Brother who ranks high in the estimation of the
brethren, and now fills the first office in the Grand
Lodge of England under his royal highness the
Prince of Wales."]—(*Masonic Library*, vol. i. pp. 363,
364.) The paragraph in brackets is not in Oliver's
Reprint of Preston, but in the London twelfth ed.,
1812, p. 244.

Here we find "*irregularities continued to prevail*, and
several worthy brethren still adverse" became "highly
disgusted" at the "encroachments on the established
system of the institution." These "irregularities" were
among the Masons under the London Grand Lodge.
The *encroachments* must have been of a serious nature
to disgust *worthy brethren*. What the encroachments
were on the established system, no writer has informed

us. We only know the irregularities prevailed among the London Lodges. It was those worthy brethren who, highly disgusted, left their Lodges and joined the York Masons, whom the London Masons stigmatized as seceders. We cannot wonder that the London craft were largely infected with disgust at the continued encroachments, and that therefore there were constant complaints, and that the communications of the Grand Lodge were "fully employed in adjusting differences and reconciling animosities." How the Grand Lodge succeeded in its efforts in harmonizing its own members and reconciling those opposed to its encroachments on the established system is manifest in *more secessions taking place*. The Grand Lodge then found it necessary to take some action. It passed votes of censure and enacted laws to discourage irregular associations; but all this effected nothing; they were dead enactments; those whom it intended to reach were no longer under its jurisdiction. But Preston, copying Anderson, Entick & Co., goes on in the same old strain, the often repeated tale over again, of Lodges formed without legal warrants, persons initiated contrary to the laws, for small and unworthy considerations, &c., all referring to Ancient York Lodges regularly constituted and their members.

If we view the action of the London Grand Lodge as taken from Preston, from a true Masonic standpoint, without bias or being deceived by the specious inferences of the writer, no other conclusion can be come to than that the "altercations," "general mur-

mur," "dissatisfied brethren having separated themselves," &c., were caused by the *Innovations of the
London Masons* in the secret signs and tokens, which
justly "*offended* many old Masons*" who united with
Lodges holding under the jurisdiction of the York
Grand Lodge, of which, no doubt, more or less were
established long prior to the revolution of the London
Masons in 1717, and who continued their regular
meetings down to and subsequent to 1739, when the
occurrences mentioned took place. It is a wicked
assumption that the Lodges held meetings and initiated persons into Masonry, and without authority
assumed the character of York Masons. The "irregularities" mentioned to attach odium to those worthy
brethren adverse to the encroachments on the established system of the institution by the London Grand
Lodge, were sufficient to "highly disgust" true and
"worthy brethren," and good cause for leaving an
organization guilty of the criminal offence of violating
their obligations in changing the secret work of Masonry. The "irregularities" were all on the side of
the London Masons; they were the originators of
them, of innovations, encroachments, aggressions,
and seceding from the established system of Masonry;
and it was not only the duty but obligatory on those
"worthy brethren," as Masons, to leave that organization. They would not have been true to the institution, to themselves, to their covenants, if they had
only in appearance, by continuing their relations,
given the semblance of acquiescence to their unlawful
proceedings. It was no wonder that "more seces-

sions took place," and that "lodges were formed
without any legal warrant" from the London Grand
Lodge. As to the "enacting laws to discourage irregular associations of the Fraternity," we will show
in the course of these reviews that those *irregular
associations*, as they are conveniently termed by the
London Grand Lodge, were regular bodies of York
Masons which the London Grand Lodge, with all
its powers, penal enactments, stringent regulations,
changing the modes of recognition, and studied efforts
to defame and attach stigma to, could not get the
York Masons nor their own members, who in disgust
left them and affiliated with the York Masons, to recognize the irregularities, innovations, and infractions
of the established system of Masonry by the London
craft. The specious reasoning employed to make it
appear that the associations referred to were irregular
is too glaringly inconsistent not to be noticed by the
intelligent reader. Of course, the London Masons
would insist that the "lodges were formed without
legal warrants," because they did not emanate from
their own Grand Lodge. The statement that "the
Grand Lodge *readily* acquiesced in the imprudent
measures which the regular Masons had adopted,"
was a mean evasion of truth to make it appear that
the changes made " to distinguish the persons initiated
by them " did not originate with the Grand Lodge.
It must have originated in the governing body, or
else it would have taken prompt measures to prevent
so gross an offence as the violation of most solemn
obligations binding upon all Masons. That was a

measure of expediency which none but the most vile
and corrupt would be guilty of. We do not believe
that the "imprudent measures" adopted by the Grand
Lodge "had the intended effect." The statement was
made to make it appear that the independency declared and assuming the appellation of *ancient* Masons
resulted in those brethren instituting "a new Grand
Lodge." Entick, who published the Constitutions in
1756, does not mention the establishment of a *new*
Grand Lodge. We will soon examine Entick, and
copy what he reports on the subject of the "Ancient
Masons."

We remind the reader of what we have written in
foregoing pages in regard to the formation of the
London Grand Lodge, the prior encroachments of
the London Masons, and usurpations of the prerogatives inherent in the Grand Lodge at York, and the
subsequent acts of violations of Masonic comity and
persistent silence as to the existence of the legitimate
Mother Grand Lodge from which they derived their
original Masonic Constitutions and Masonic establishment. We need not repeat that the London
Grand Lodge was formed without authority, without
precedent, and simply by "assuming independency."
It did not therefore become it, even if its declara-
tions of "irregular associations" were true, which
they were not, in casting odium and untruthful
reflections upon "worthy brethren" and their as-
sociates for declaring their independency and
assuming the distinctive title "*Ancient Masons*," a
title they always possessed. The appellation "*Mod-*

ern Masons," the London Masons by their conduct
seemed to court. They appeared to desire to abro-
gate all ancient Masonry, its laws, customs, usages,
and its fundamental principles, and therefore the
title Modern Masons was rightly given them. We
had the subject of difference explained to us a third
of a century ago by the intelligent Mason Z. A.
Davis, whilst conferring the degrees on us. At present little is said and less known of the history, origin,
or cause of the different titles applied to Masons,
but in teaching and examination, Ancient York Masons is the term still in use in most jurisdictions.
But that the London Masons merited the title of
modern there can be no question. It is a gratuitous
assertion that the York Masons in London instituted
a new Grand Lodge at London. The sovereign
body existed at York, it had Lodges established in
many places in England as well as at London, and
many Masons made under the jurisdiction of the London Grand Lodge left and came under the banner of
the York Masons. It was not a *new* Grand Lodge
established at London, although, in consequence of
the increase of Lodges and members, authority may
have been given to execute some of the functions of
a Grand Lodge, as District or Provincial, by the
Grand Lodge of York. It is in the light of these
remarks the above statements must be read.

Preston in his qualified statement, "they instituted
a *new* Grand Lodge in London, *professedly* on the
Ancient system," subsequently remarks in same paragraph : "The irregular Masons in London having thus

acquired a nominal establishment, noblemen of both kingdoms unacquainted with the origin of separation, honored them with their patronage," &c. That fully agrees with our views that no third Grand Lodge was formed in England. Neither Entick nor Blaney mention such an organization. Preston's remarks refer to 1739. Both Entick and Elaney only speak of Ancient Masons in 1754, and in no other place. As we have already quoted the whole paragraph, we here remark that Preston relies too much upon the supposed ignorance of the noblemen of both kingdoms, Scotland and Ireland, of being unacquainted with the origin of what he calls the separation. There is ingenuity and deceit in Preston's remarks. The nominal establishment was, as we have intimated, a regular appointment by the York Grand Lodge, as subsequent remarks will prove. And the *fallacy* detected in the same paragraph did not change the views of the Scots and Irish Masons, as it was more than sixty years afterwards before they entered into correspondence with the London Masons. Preston is better authority than Anderson, Entick, or Oliver, although an independent judgment should be formed, making due allowance for the influences surrounding Preston during his Masonic life. It would seem to be imposing upon the intelligence or credulity of readers to believe that " worthy brethren," " many gentlemen of reputation," and " the Scots and Irish Masons," could be deceived by any representations made, which, if not true, could be readily ascertained as being so near home.

In continuation of the London Grand Lodge, the "Earl of Kintore succeeded Lord Raymond as Grand Master, 1740, and in imitation of his predecessor, continued to discourage irregularities." The Earl of Morton succeeded as Grand Master, 1741. Lord Ward succeeded the Earl of Morton as Grand Master, April 27, 1742, who "lost no time in applying effectual remedies to *reconcile* the animosities which prevailed." "Many lodges, which were in a declining state, by his advice, *coalesced* with others in better circumstances; some, which had been negligent in their attendance on the Communications, after proper admonitions, were restored to favor; and others, which persevered in their contumacy, were erased out of the list." Lord Ward was continued Grand Master two years. "The unanimity and harmony of the lodges seemed to be perfectly restored under his lordship's administration." "He was succeeded by the Earl of Strathmore." "Lord Cranstoun was elected Grand Master in April, 1745, and presided over the Fraternity with great reputation two years. Under his auspices Masonry flourished." "Lord Byron succeeded 1747, and was Grand Master five years. Lord Carysford succeeded as Grand Master 1752, and served two years. The Marquis of Carnarvon succeeded as Grand Master 1754. He ordered the Book of Constitutions to be reprinted. Soon after his election, the Grand Lodge took into consideration a complaint against certain brethren for assembling without *any* legal authority, under the denomination of *Ancient Masons*, and who as such considered them-

selves independen* of the Society, and not subject to
the laws of the Grand Lodge, or to the control of the
Grand Master. Dr. Manningham, the Deputy Grand
Master, pointed out the necessity of discouraging
such meetings, as being contrary to the laws of the
Society, and openly subversive of the allegiance due
the Grand Master. On this representation the Grand
Lodge resolved, that the meeting of any brethren
under the denomination of Masons, other than as
brethren of the ancient and honorable Society of
Free and Accepted Masons, established upon the universal system, is inconsistent with the honour and interest of the Craft, and a high insult on the Grand
Master and the whole body of Masons. In consequence of this resolution, fourteen brethren, who are
members of a lodge held at the Ben Johnson's head,
in Pelham street, Spitalfields, were expelled the Society, and the lodge was ordered to be erased out of
the list." Preston says : " No preceding Grand Master granted so many provincial deputations as the
Marquis of Carnarvon. On the 7th of October, 1755,
his lordship appointed a Provincial Grand Master for
Durham, and soon after *a very respectable lodge* was
constituted at Sunderland, under his lordship's auspices."

The fuss and bluster of Dr. Manningham, and the
adoption of a resolution against the Ancient Masons,
" who as such considered themselves independent of
the society and not subject to the laws of the Grand
Lodge," eventuated, all in the same paragraph, in
expelling fourteen members and the erasure of the

Lodge out of the list. The Lodge therefore consisted of only fourteen members. Here Preston makes Dr. Manningham give the title of "the ancient and honorable Society of the Free and Accepted Masons established upon the Universal system," to the London Body. Entick does not give that title, hence Preston interpolated. The transactions took place in 1755, and Entick's Book of Constitutions was published in 1756. Entick does not say how many were expelled, only that Lodge No. 94 "be erased out of the Book of Lodges." The name and place of meeting of that Lodge is not in Anderson's list published in 1738. The No. 94 of Anderson was constituted August 24, 1737, and met at the Gun Tavern in Jermyn Street, St. James. Entick's No. 94 met at the Ben Johnson's Head in Pelham Street, Spital-Fields. Who can reconcile these differences? One or the other or both must be false. Entick, however, would not mention the small number of members of that Lodge, or the Grand Lodge would not permit him. But is not the whole statement of the action and resolution of the Grand Lodge a fabrication made up for effect? And did not Preston interpolate to make the false statement seem probable? In adding to the title, Preston falsified himself, according to extracts in previous pages. He well knew that the London Grand Lodge did not apply the word Ancient to its title, and he also knew that it was not "established upon the Universal system." But believing that if there was any truth in the statements of Entick, that Lodge No. 94 was erased out of the list, it could not have been a Lodge

constituted by the London Grand Lodge, and therefore was not under its jurisdiction.   The remarks,
then, that the "Ancient Masons, who, as such, consider themselves as independent of this Society, and
not subject to our Laws, or to the Authority of our
Grand Master," were simply gratuitous, of no effect,
not applicable to the Lodge or its members who were
not under its Constitutions, owed it no allegiance,
were not bound by its Laws, and not subject to the
Authority of its Grand Master.   The reader cannot
fail to perceive that in all the notices of the London
Grand Lodge of irregular Masons, of expulsions and
erasures of Lodges, there .was an object persistently
kept in view, to ignore the existence of the York
Grand Lodge, of Lodges under its authority, and to
hold out the inference that *it* was the only legal Masonic authority existing in the kingdom.

We now turn to Entick's Constitutions, commencing from the close of Anderson's Constitutions, and
note only such matters as pertain to our subject.

Grand Lodge, June 30, 1739.   Lord Raymond,
Grand Master.   They "proceeded to examine a complaint exhibited against certain Brethren, suspected
of being concerned in an irregular making of Masons;
but did not go through with this inquiry, it being
postponed to some other opportunity."

Grand Lodge, December 12, 1739.   "And having
finished their inquiry into the irregularities complained of at the last Communication, and pardoned
the transgressors, upon their submission and promises
of future good behaviour, it was Ordered, That the

laws be strictly put in execution against all such brethren as shall for the future countenance, connive, or assist at any irregular makings."

Grand Lodge, June, 1740. Earl of Kintore, Grand Master. "Three of the late Stewards were complained of for being present and assisting at irregular makings."

Grand Lodge, June 24, 1742. Lord Ward, Grand Master. "The Master of the Turk's Head Lodge in Greek street, Soho, acquainted the Grand Master, that, as the said Lodge was greatly declined, he and the members had joined the King's Arms Lodge No. 38, held at the Cannon, Charing Cross; and that by consent of the said Turk's Head Lodge, he did surrender the Constitution thereof to his Worship. For which they were much applauded by the Grand Master, as worthy of example, where Lodges were in a declining irretrievable state. Ordered, That the lodge No. 37, at the Angel and Crown, in Whitechapel; No. 60, at the Vine, in Long Acre; No. 161, at the Swan, on Fish Street Hill, be erased out of the list, and be no longer esteemed regular lodges, for not attending the Grand Master in Quarterly Communications pursuant to several notices sent them respectively."

Grand Lodge, February 8, 1743. "Were highly satisfied with the conduct of the Lodge No. 47, held at the Rose in Cheapside, who, finding their state in great decline, had joined themselves to the Swan and Rummer, and surrendered their Constitution to the Grand Master at the Communication."

Grand Lodge, April 9, 1743. "Ordered, That the lodges No. 40, at the Globe, in Fleet street; No. 45, at the Globe, in the Strand; No. 59, at the Castle, in St. Giles; No. 80, at the Three Tuns, in Grosvenor street; No. 145, at the Three Tuns and Half Moon, on Snow Hill; No. 156, at the Red Lion, in Red Lion street; No. 165, at the Flower Pot, in Bishops-gate street, should be immediately erased out of the list of regular lodges, for not attending the Grand Master in Quarterly Communication, pursuant to several notices sent them respectively."

Grand Lodge, April 4, 1744. "Ordered, That the lodges, No. 7, at the King's Arms, Temple Bar, No. 39, at the Mitre, in King street, Westminster, should be immediately erased out of the list of regular lodges for not obeying the summons of the Grand Master to attend him in Quarterly Communication."

Grand Lodge, February 26, 1745. Earl of Strath-more, Grand Master. "The Master and Wardens of Lodge 185, lately held at the Three Tuns in Hough-ton street, Clare Market, surrendered their Constitu-tion to the Grand Master; the Brethren having agreed to join the lodge No. 102 at the Magpye and Horse-shoe, in Hollis street, near Clare Market."

Grand Lodge, March 25, 1745. "It was Ordered, That the following lodges, not attending according to the summons sent by order of the last Quarterly Communication, should be erazed out of the Book of Lodges, viz.: No. 3, the Crown, behind the Royal Ex-change; No. 9, the King's Arms, in New Bond street, (subsequently restored;) No. 17, the Sun, in Holborn;

No. 19, the Vine, in Long Acre; No. 26, Forrest's Coffee-house, Charing Cross; No. 146, the King's Head, in the Old Jewry; No. 159, the Gloucester Lodge, at the Cannon, Charing Cross; No. 173, the British Coffee-house, Charing Cross."

Grand Lodge, November 21, 1745. Lord Cranstoun, Grand Master. "Ordered, The twelve following lodges to be erased out of the Book of Lodges, they not having attended the Grand Master at the General Meetings of the Society, nor regularly met so as to be summoned for some years, viz.: No. 15, the Bedford Arms, in Covent Garden; No. 16, the Bear and Rummer, in Gerard street, Soho; No. 25, the Dog, in St. James' Market; No. 48, the Royal Oak, in Earl street, Seven Dials; No. 54, the George, in St. Mary Axe, (subsequently restored;) No. 79, the King's Head, in St. Paul's Church-yard; No. 107, the Fountain, on Snow Hill; No. 112, the Horn and Dolphin, in Crutched Friars; No. 142, the White Horse, in Piccadilly; No. 160, the Horn and Feathers, in Doctors' Commons; No. 171, the Standard, in Leicester Fields; No. 155, the Mansion House, near the Steelyard, in Thames street."

Grand Lodge, April 14, 1746. "Ordered, That the four following lodges be erazed out of the Book of Lodges for non-attendance, according to the order of the last Quarterly Communication, viz.: No. 33, the Sash and Cocoa-Tree, in Moorfields; No. 88, the Hoop and Griffin, in Leadenhall street; No. 140, the King's Arms, in Cateaton street; No. 153, the Fountain, in Bartholomew Lane."

Grand Lodge, December 22, 1748. Lord Byron, Grand Master. "Ordered, That the Lodges No. 41, at Mount's Coffee-house, in Grosvenor street; No. 70, at the Salutation, in Newgate street; No. 83, at the Sun, in Ludgate street; No. 125, at Ashley's London Punch-house; No. 143, at the Swan, in Southwark, be erazed out of the Book of Lodges for non-attendance, when summoned by order of the Grand Master to meet him in Quarterly Communication. The Lodge held at the White Bear, in old Broad street, having declined, the Master, by the consent of the other members, surrendered the Constitution into the hands of the Grand Master."

Grand Lodge, November 30, 1752. Baron of Carysfort, Grand Master. "It was ordered, That the Lodges No. 89, at the Angel and Crown, near St. Agnes le Clare, in Hoxton; No. 90, at the Royal Vineyard, in St. James' Park; No. 106, at Forrest's Coffee-house, Charing Cross, be erazed out of the Book of Lodges, they not having attended the Quarterly Communications, or other meetings of the Society, or paid any charity for upwards of five years past."

Grand Lodge, June 27, 1754. James Brydges, Marquis of Carnarvon, Grand Master. "They took into consideration the state of the country lodges; and it was Resolved, That each Brother should, according to his opportunity, make the utmost enquiry touching the meetings and conduct of said lodges, and give proper intimations thereof to the next Quarterly Communication. And that such of those lodges, of which no satisfactory account could be then given, should be erazed from the Book of Lodges."

Grand Lodge, November 29, 1754. "Ordered, That the following *twenty-one* lodges, having neither contributed to the general fund of charity, nor otherwise had any communication with the Grand Lodge, nor even met for several years, according to the best information that could be obtained, be erazed out of the Book of Regular Lodges, viz.: No. 32, Red Lion, at Congleton in Cheshire; No. 42, King's Head, at Salford, near Manchester; No. 46, Woolpack, at Warwick; No. 52, Three Tuns, at Scarborough; No. 57, St. Rook's Hill, near Chichester; No. 58, Red Lion, at Canterbury; No. 64, George, at Northampton; No. 71, Fleece, at Bury St. Edmunds; No. 77, Bell and Dove, at Woolverhampton; No. 86, New Inn, at Exeter; No. 96, Seven Stars, at Bury St. Edmunds; No. 119, Mason's Arms, at Oswestree; No. 121, Lord Weymouth's Arms, at Warminster; No. 128, Fountain, at Shrewsbury; No. 130, Three Crowns, at Weymouth; No. 141, Horn, at Braintree; No. 151, Angel above Hill, in the Bailiwick of Lincoln; No. 152, Swan and Dove, at Hereford; No. 163, Swan at Tewksbury; No. 175, Black Bull, at Spalding." Entick only names twenty lodges.

Grand Lodge, March 20, 1755. "The Grand Lodge then took into consideration a complaint against certain Brethren for forming and assembling under the denomination of a lodge of *Ancient Masons*, who, as such, consider themselves as independent of this Society, and not subject to our Laws, or to the

Authority of our Grand Master. When the Deputy Grand Master took notice of the great necessity there was to discourage all such meetings, not only as the same were contrary to our laws, and a great insult on the Grand Master, and the whole body of Free and Accepted Masons: But as they likewise tended to introduce into the Craft the novelties and conceits of opinionative persons, and to create a belief that there have been other Societies of Masons more ancient than that of *this* ancient and honorable Society."

The complaint here made against certain brethren can only cause a smile at its continued repetition and the futility of all such efforts as the Grand Lodge had made against Masons who owed it no allegiance. Especially so and ridiculous in the extreme when it asserts that *they* "*consider* themselves as independent of this Society, not subject to our laws or to the authority of our Grand Master." *They consider themselves,* — of course they had a right to judge for themselves, why not? Did the Grand Lodge want to exercise judgment for them? Such an assumption of arrogance and presumption might be exercised upon bondmen or such as possess no gleam of intelligence, but not upon Masons. They were not subject to their laws nor authority, and yet they want to compel them to come under their authority, but they considered for themselves and did n't. But the Deputy Grand Master rises to the height of arrogant effrontery. What! to doubt that this Society, formed in 1717, is not the most ancient body of Masons!

What assurance, to "create a belief that there have been other Societies of Masons more ancient than that of *this* ancient and honorable Society." The author of that striking declaration was the celebrated Dr. Manningham, and made before the London Grand Lodge, March 20, 1755. Preston, with better knowledge, omits the last quotation, although he copies nearly the whole article. We might extend our remarks on the adoption of the resolution offered, but we forbear.

"And, the question being put, That the meeting of any Brethren of this Society, as, or under any denomination of Masons, other than as Brethren of this our ancient and honourable Society of Free and Accepted Masons, is inconsistent with the honour and interests of the Craft, and a high insult on our Grand Master, and the whole body of Masons: It was carried in the affirmative; one (?) of the Brethren complained of, only dissenting. The Deputy Grand Master, in his great clemency, then moved, That the consideration of the irregular proceedings of the said Brethren might be postponed till next Quarterly Communication, hoping that a thorough sense of their misconduct, and a determination not to be guilty of the like for the future, would then appear and reconcile them to the Grand Lodge."

Grand Lodge, July 24, 1755. "Ordered, That the Brethren complained of at the last Quarterly Communication, persisting in their disobedience to the determination of the Grand Lodge, their Lodge No. 94, held at the Ben Johnson's Head, in Pelham street,

Spital-Fields, be erazed from the Book of Lodges; and that such of the Brethren thereof, who shall continue those irregular meetings, be not admitted as visitors in any Lodge." Here closes Entick's 1756 ed. of the Book of Constitutions. A remarkable feature to be noticed is the large number of Lodges erased from the Book of Lodges, their peculiar names indicating the places of meeting and the surrounding associations.

In all the notices of complaints of "irregular meetings of Brethren," "of irregular lodges," and the proceedings of the Grand Lodge, there is no mention of a new Grand Lodge established by the Ancient Masons in either Anderson's, Entick's, or Blaney's 1767 Constitutions. Preston is the only authority, and he only mentions in 1739, "They instituted a *new* Grand Lodge in London, *professedly* on the *ancient* system." There would seem to be a doubt in the above statement of Preston. Besides Oliver, who wrote nearly one hundred years afterwards, and reprinted Preston, and the above remark, there is no authority for the assertion that there was a *third* Grand Lodge instituted in England; certainly none in any authorized Grand Lodge publication. There is frequent mention of "irregular meetings," "irregular lodges," "irregular Masons" and "Brethren," but not of a *new* Grand Lodge; and the Grand Lodge at York could not have been meant, as that body was in existence before the London Grand Lodge was formed. Besides, Preston, whenever the York Grand Lodge is mentioned by him, he does not mention it in connection with irıegular Lodges or Masons. The intention of the London Grand Lodge was to make it appear that those irregular Lodges, so called, were *isolated assemblages* under no regular Masonic authority. We re-assert that all those Masons and assemblages under the ban of the London Grand Lodge as " irregular," were Lodges and Masons under the jurisdiction of the York Grand Lodge, were regular made Masons, and were made in Lodges regularly constituted. We deny that there is any authentic proof to the contrary, or any proof whatever, of authority, that a new Grand Lodge was instituted in England after the irregular Grand Lodge was formed in London in 1717. We have the best evidence, and confirmatory of our views, that those so-called irregular meetings were Lodges of York Masons, in the fact that the irregular body formed in 1717 does not mention or refer to the Grand Lodge at York from whence they as Masons originally derived their authority, and which was in existence at that time, except the false and malicious statement of Anderson in its " affecting independency," — calling it, " *the old Lodge at York City*," under the heading of " Deputations sent beyond Sea," thus placing it out of the jurisdiction of England, and for no other purpose than to deceive and mislead.

The Anderson Constitutions will not bear close criticism. Why place the old York Lodge under the caption of deputations *beyond* the Sea ? Why mention it under the deputations at all ? Why call it the old Lodge at York City? These are pertinent questions; and the only inferences to be drawn from Anderson's inserting the paragraph already quoted, and including Scotland, Ireland, France, and Italy in connection with the old Lodge at York City under the heading referred to, was the intention to mislead the reader and represent that there was no Grand Lodge at York City.

Anderson publishes, in the 1738 Constitutions, "A List of the Lodges in and about London and Westminster," numbering from *one consecutive to one hundred and six*, giving the names, "Signs of the Houses" where meeting, "Dates of Constitution," and " Days of Forming," and has the following observations: " Many Lodges have by accident broken up, or are partitioned, or else removed to new places for their conveniency, and so, if subsisting, they are called and known by those new places or their signs. But the subsisting Lodges, whose officers have attended the Grand Lodge or Quarterly Communication, and brought their benevolence to the Grand Charity within twelve months past, *are here set down according to seniority of Constitution, as in the Grand Lodge Books and the engraven list.*" (See *Masonic Library*, pp. 669-672, vol. ii.)

It would seem, from the numbering, names, dates of Constitution taken from the Books of the Grand Lodge and the *engraven* list,—which engraven list was renewed annually with their removals, — that there could not possibly be an error, and that reference to it would be conclusive authority. In, however, comparing Entick's " List of Regular Lodges according to their Seniority and Constitution, by order of the

Grand Master," we find so wide a difference as to cause the gravest doubts of the correctness and reliability of both constitutions. Entick has up to the close of 1738 only 101 Lodges, Anderson 106. There are but 8 Lodges of the whole number in Entick which agree with Anderson, yet these two lists are taken from the same records, the same authority. Entick has the names, places, days of meeting, and times of constitution, (but not numbered,) of 210 Lodges constituted from 1721 to 1756 inclusive, and including 43 instituted in America, the West Indies, and in different countries in Europe, leaving 167 lodges in England under the jurisdiction of the London Grand Lodge, a gain of 61 lodges from 1738. But more remarkable than the difference mentioned in the two lists, and the circumstance that only 8 lodges are mentioned which are the same in the two lists, is that the Grand Lodge erased from its Books *ten* lodges in 1742 and 1743, giving the number, name, and place of meeting of each, so that by referring to Entick, pp. 240, 241, these lodges can be identified. Entick gives the number of lodges up to the *close of* 1743, (less 20 foreign lodges,) 106 in England. Among the lodges erased as before noticed, 1742 and 1748, were lodges numbered 145, 156, 161, 165.

As the Grand Lodge numbered no doubt consecutive, and as there were, including the 20 foreign lodges, 120 altogether, there could be no lodges of numbers above 126. There is a discrepancy here which no mathematician can adjust. On comparing Anderson's list of 106 lodges with Entick's to the close of 1738, there are *not ten lodges which are the same in both.* The two authorized Books cannot be reconciled, therefore, neither can be considered authority, notwithstanding the approval of the Grand Masters, Grand Officers, respectable committees, and the final approval of the Grand Lodges, and authorizing with their approbation these two Books of Constitutions. These irreconcilable discrepant publications, to the intelligent investigating mind, would prove that either the Grand Lodge records were imperfectly kept, or the author was, purposely by Grand Lodge authority, *instructed* to falsify the truth in order to deceive the public. But what of the Book of Lodges and the Engraven List? Was not the whole matter of these publications got up for a purpose? Anderson was the author of the 1723 and 1738 Constitutions, and he was assisted by Desaguliers and Payne. These were the active agents in the formation of the London Grand Lodge; the men who led the crowd, and who worked in accord to gain their end. There could not have been 165 lodges in 1743. Entick copied, it is assumed, from the record. The proceedings in Grand Lodge give the numbers of the lodges erased. So far we can understand. If the Book contains a correct transcript from the record, then the record is not true. Was it altered for the purpose? There were 63 lodges erased from the Books, and 5 declined merging into other lodges, making 68 lodges that from 1742 to 1756 were erased from the Books of the London Grand Lodge. It can hardly be supposed that the Grand Lodge could have been very particular as to the kind of material that the lodges were composed of, as it was not as to their places of meeting, and perhaps the only consideration was the contributions and the fees for constituting as well as to show a degree of prosperity in the increase of Lodges.

To erase sixty-eight lodges in fourteen years out of one hundred and sixty-seven lodges shows a demoralized state of things, a condition unparalleled in the history of Masonic organizations. The continued complaints made in Grand Lodge of irregular assemblies and irregular makings of Masons in lodges, in contravention of the laws of the Grand Lodge, and the persistence notwithstanding of those Lodges to hold their meetings and make Masons, proves at least that they were not under the jurisdiction of the London Grand Lodge, and therefore not subject to its laws. As they were organized bodies, they must have held authority under some Grand Lodge jurisdiction; they could not have been isolated assemblies, each independent of the others; they were a united body of Masons, and more harmonious than the craft under the jurisdiction of the London Grand Lodge. These lodges, as we have already stated, were under the jurisdiction of the York Grand Lodge, and continued so until the union in 1813. It was because they were regular lodges, Masonically constituted by the Grand Lodge at York, and because of their numbers and the very general esteem in which their Mother Grand Lodge was held as the original

and only legal source of Masonic authority, that the
London Grand Lodge did not, dared not take efficient
measures to cause them to dissolve their associations,
to discontinue making Masons and discontinue their
meetings.   If the records of Anderson are correct, if
his statements are true, the London Grand Lodge had
the power and the influence in high places to cause
those "irregular" assemblies to dissolve if they were
composed of a "few Brethren" and held their meetings without any legal Masonic authority.   But these
efficient measures were not taken, and a ruse resorted
to to prevent the members of the York Lodges from
meeting and fraternizing with the members of their
own Lodges, which we have already referred to.   That
ruse, although condemned by Preston and others,
and which could not be justified under any circumstances, Entick does not even mention.   But the
Grand Lodge (London) was very uneasy, "complaints
were preferred at every succeeding Committee, and
the communications fully employed in adjusting differences and reconciling animosities."   This of course
refers solely to the members of lodges holding under
their own (London) Grand Lodge.

The efforts of the Grand Lodge to adjust and reconcile, however, proved unavailing, as, "more secessions taking place, it became necessary to pass votes
of censure on the most refractory, and enact laws to
discourage irregular associations of the fraternity."
These "refractory" members affiliated with Lodges
of York Masons.   They were considered refractory
because they would not stultify themselves as Masons,

they would not violate their conscience in acting contrary to obligations voluntarily assumed, they would not countenance an innovation in the secret work of Masonry, which was a cause of great grief to the Grand Lodge, and hence the "votes of censure, &c.," which did not harm them nor change their character as good and true Masons. Their secession was from a body guilty of the grossest moral and Masonic wrong, and uniting with those in whom the pure principles of Masonry were conserved, the Masons holding under the York Grand Lodge. These York Masons were not amenable to nor bound by the laws of the London Grand Lodge; they held to the old Constitutions, the Charges, Landmarks, and teachings of legitimate Masonry as they had received them unchanged, unaltered, therefore they could not affiliate nor hold Masonic communion with the Masons under the London Grand Lodge. The cause for striking off from the Books of the Grand Lodge full two-fifths of its Lodges between 1742 and 1756 proves more than is written, more than we can notice. Lodges were evidently constituted by the London Grand Lodge without inquiry as to the fitness of the applicants as Masons to govern and rule a Masonic Lodge, without examination as to their Masonic acquirements, or being particular as to their places of meeting, or their moral characters and standing as men in their several communities, or regard to numbers. To multiply Lodges was the aim of the Grand Lodge, indifferent as to the material and without any considerations for the good of Masonry or the Ma-

sonic institution.   Hence the demoralized condition
of the Lodges instituted by it, the defection of its
members, the constant complaints in Grand Lodge
having more for their object a return by it to the old
institutions, to the ancient usages, customs, and Landmarks, than noticing irregularities in the Lodges of
which the Grand Lodge itself was the primary cause.

But the dissatisfaction did not cease with the erasure
of so many Lodges ; an element of disquiet still remained, a desire among honest and true Masons
among the Lodges constituted by the London Grand
Lodge to return again to the old system, and abandon
the innovations the Grand Lodge had sanctioned.

We now come to Blaney's Constitutions, published
1767, following the records of the London Grand
Lodge after Entick, 1756.   We apply the same remarks to this publication as to Anderson's and
Entick's.   It is in the same style as the others, does
not mention the York Grand Lodge, and its minutes
are as brief as its predecessors, and equally unreliable.

Grand Lodge, January 14, 1757.   The Marquis of
Carnarvon, Grand Master.   " The Grand Lodge received information that fourteen persons (names
given) who are not Masons (among others) meet the
first and third Tuesdays in every month, at the Marl-
borough Head, in Pelham street, Spital-Fields, and
hold what they call a lodge.   Ordered, That a list of
their names be printed, and sent to every lodge, that
they may be on their guard in their respective lodges,
lest any of those impostors should gain admittance
among them.   Ordered, That the Grand Secretary

send notice to the seven following lodges, to attend at the next Quarterly Communication, and show cause why they have not attended the General Meetings of the Society for some time past, viz.: No. 61, Red Cross Barbican; No. 62, Putney, Bowling Green; No. 75, King's Arms, St. Margaret's Hill; No. 129, Rising Sun, Fashion street; No. 144, Three Tuns, Spital-Fields; No. 230, Queen's Head, Great Queen street; No. 246, Crown, at Cripplegate."

Grand Lodge, May 5, 1757. "It was ordered that the three following lodges, not having attended to the Summons of the last Quarterly Communication, be erased out of the list of lodges: No. 75, King's Arms, St. Margaret's Hill; No. 129, Rising Sun, in Fashion street, Spital-Fields; No. 230, Queen's Head, Great Queen street, Lincoln's Inn Fields. The four other lodges summoned by order of the last Quarterly Communication attended and were excused."

Grand Lodge, October 31, 1757. "Ordered, That the three lodges lately held at the King's Arms, St. Margaret's Hill, the Rising Sun, in Fashion street, Spital-Fields, and the Queen's Head in Great Queen street, and erazed from the list of lodges by order of the Quarterly Communication held the 5th of May, 1757, having *paid two guineas each*, be, at their desire, restored and entered again on the list."

Grand Lodge, February 14, 1758. "Ordered, That No. 106, at King William's Head, at Portsmouth, and No. 160, the Blackmoor's Head, at Nottingham, be erazed from the list of lodges, no lodges having met at either of those places for a considerable time."

Grand Lodge, February 5, 1759. "The lodge No. 32, at the George, in St. Mary Axe, having represented that they had not a sufficient number of members to hold a lodge: Ordered, That for the future they be omitted in the list of lodges."

Grand Lodge, November 17, 1760. Among the Grand Officers and Provincial Grand Master of Calcutta, East Indies, present, the record continues — "Franklyn, Esq., Provincial Grand Master of Philadelphia; — Franklyn, Esq., Provincial Grand Secretary of Philadelphia." "Notice being sent to the following lodges to show cause for their non-attendance at the Quarterly Communication, Dog Tavern, Garlick Hill, Crown in Smithfield, St. Paul's, Spright's Town, Barbadoes, Swan, Westminster Bridge, Hoop and Grapes, St. Martin's Lane, Gateshead in the County of Durham, Saracen's Head at Lincoln, no Brother appearing for them, they were ordered to be erazed out of the list of lodges."

Grand Lodge, June 5, 1761. "A Brother present acquainted the Grand Lodge that at the Glaziers Arms, in Water Lane, Fleet street, several persons meet there who for small and unworthy considerations make Masons in a clandestine manner. Ordered, That as soon as the names of the persons so meeting can be obtained, they shall be printed and sent to all the regular lodges in London, and whoever appears to be the acting Master and Wardens, be expelled all lodges, and the others not admitted into any regular lodge."

Grand Lodge, March 29, 1762. "It was reported

that, agreeable to the order of the last Quarterly
Communication, the names of those persons who
meet at the Glaziers Arms in Water Lane, Fleet
street, had been sent to all the lodges." "The following lodges not having attended for a considerable
time at any Quarterly Communication, it was ordered
that letters be sent to them, desiring them to show
cause at the next Quarterly Communication for their
former non-attendance; otherwise they should be
erased out of the list of lodges; viz.: Grapes, at
Chatham; Horn, Fleet street; Salutation, Nicholas
Lane; Three Tuns, Spital-Fields; Three Tuns, Ald-
gate; Swan, Grafton street, Soho; Bear, Lemon
street, Goodman's Fields; Horn, Doctors' Commons;
King's Arms, Queenbythe."

Grand Lodge, July 27, 1762. "Notice having been
sent to the following lodges, to shew cause for their
non-attendance at the Quarterly Communications, no
Brother appearing for them, they were ordered to be
erased out of the list of lodges; viz.: The Horn Tavern,
Fleet street; Bear, Lemon street, Goodman's Fields."

Grand Lodge, October 24, 1763. "The following
lodges not having attended for a considerable time at
any Quarterly Communication, it was ordered, that
letters be sent to them desiring them to shew cause,
at the next Quarterly Communication, for their former non-attendance, otherwise they should be erased
out of the list of lodges; viz.: King's Arms, New
Bond street; Golden Anchor, Greenwich; Fountain,
Shoreditch; Blue Posts, Southampton Buildings; Angel, Picadilly; White Hart, Mansfield street, Goodman's Fields."

Grand Lodge, January 23, 1764. "The Quarterly Communication ordered the following lodges to be erased out of the list of lodges for their non-attendance at the Quarterly Communications; viz.: King's Arms, New Bond street; Fountain, Shoreditch; White Hart, Mansfield street, Goodman's Fields; Two Blue Posts, Southampton Buildings."

Grand Lodge, April 23, 1764. "The petition of several Brethren, late members of the King's Arms Lodge, in New Bond street, praying to be reinstated, was read: The Quarterly Communication ordered, upon their paying two guineas, they should stand in the same rank in the list of lodges as before."

Grand Lodge, October 29, 1765. "The memorial of several Brethren, late at the Fountain in Shoreditch, praying to be restored, was read; and upon paying two guineas to the public fund of charity, were ordered to be reinstated."

As will be seen, the erasure of Lodges not only continued, but the Grand Lodge seems to have made that a matter of speculation, as upon the *payment of two guineas* they were reinstated. Lodges were erased which had not attended the Quarterly Communications for a considerable time. That indefinite period is frequently mentioned, as well as *several* Lodges, *several* brethren, which, being so clear (?) as to time and numbers, aids the close investigator so much, that his equanimity of mind could not be disturbed, however much he might feel disposed to find fault. But the following is not so clear: "The petitions of several brethren, late members of the King's Arms

Lodge, praying to be reinstated, was read. Ordered, upon their paying two guineas, they should stand in the same rank in the list of Lodges as before." As that Lodge was erased out of the list of Lodges at the prior Quarterly Communication, the warrant must have been returned to those *several* brethren, as they were restored to the same rank in the list of Lodges as before." The question is, how many were so restored, so that we can know the number to reconstitute a Lodge, because at the following Communication a memorial of *several* brethren, late of Fountain Lodge, which had been erased, praying to be restored, were simply "reinstated on the payment of two guineas." We do not know if they each paid two guineas, or if a whole Lodge, without regard to numbers, only paid two guineas. The record does not say if the warrant of Fountain Lodge was given to those several brethren or not; if not, they were by their reinstatement unaffiliated Masons. The imperfect statement of the record will be obvious as most unsatisfactory and unintelligible.

Grand Lodge, January 29, 1766. "A Brother informed the Grand Lodge, that Brother Jonathan Scott had, for a small and unworthy consideration, made William Morgan, Carpenter and Undertaker, near Clare Market, and William Bailey, at the Three Tuns, Brook street, Clare Market, Masons. Ordered, that a N. B. be put at the bottom of each summons for the next Committee of Charity, and Quarterly Communication, desiring the Lodges not to admit them as visitors."

Grand Lodge, April 9, 1766. "Brother Jonathan Scott, in obedience to the order of the last Committee of Charity, appeared, and asked public pardon for the indiscretion he had been guilty of in making Masons irregularly, and for unworthy considerations; and he producing a certificate of such Masons being since remade, and promising never to be guilty of the like again, was thereupon restored to grace."

Grand Lodge, October 17, 1766. "The following Lodges not having attended for a considerable time at any Quarterly Communication, it was ordered, that letters be sent to them, to shew cause, at the next Quarterly Communication, for their non-attendance; otherwise they will be erased out of the list of lodges: Globe, Fleet street; Red Cross Inn, Southwark; No. 85, George, Ironmonger Lane; Mercer's Arms, Mercer's street, Long Acre."

This closes the Blaney's Constitutions, so called because ordered to be published whilst he was Grand Master. There is an appendix to the Book containing a summary of the transactions of the Grand Lodge to the "Assembly and Feast," May 5, 1769. Henry, Duke of Beaufort, Grand Master. This Book does not contain a list of the Lodges, which is much to be regretted. It does not mention the Grand Lodge at York, nor the "new Grand Lodge in London professedly on the *ancient* system," mentioned by Preston. It may therefore be taken as established truth that no such Grand Lodge was formed; and the remark of Preston following, that they (meaning the New Grand

Lodge) "pretended to justify (themselves) under the feigned sanction of the Ancient York Constitution," sustains us in the opinion that the York Grand Lodge had established a District or Provincial authority at London for the convenience of the numerous lodges under its Constitution, held in the metropolis and its surrounding districts.

Preston, writing of near the close of 1760, states that "Masonry now flourished at home and abroad under the English Constitution," and lauds highly "Lord Aberdour, who continued at the head of the fraternity five years," as having "equalled any of his predecessors in the number of appointments to the office of Provincial Grand Master;" and mentions the second appointment "for the town of Norwich and county of Norfolk," "by which the Society has been *materially benefitted.* By the diligence and attention of the late Edward Bacon, Esq., to whom the patent was first granted, *the lodges in Norwich and Norfolk considerably increased,* and *Masonry was regularly conducted in that province* under his inspection for many years."

But in the next paragraph, writing only nineteen months later, he commences : "Lord Aberdour held the office of Grand Master till the 3d of May, 1762, when he was succeeded by Earl Ferrers, during whose presidency *nothing remarkable occurred.* The Society seems at this time to *have lost much of its consequence;* the general assemblies and communications not having been honored with the presence of the nobility as formerly, and many lodges erased out of the list for non-attendance on the duties of the Grand Lodge."

Here Preston has the following note. "Since this period, *new Constitutions had been too easily granted, and lodges multiplied beyond proportion.* A proper check, however, is now put to this practice, the LEG-ISLATURE having prohibited by a late Act of Parliament the constituting any new lodges." *This refers to the Act of* 1798, *thirty-six years subsequent to* 1762.

We have passed over many of such conflicting statements as the above, mentioning the flourishing state of Masonry at a certain period and a short time afterward the reverse, because we did not care to increase the size of this publication. But what does Preston mean in saying *Masonry was regularly conducted in that province?* Does he insinuate that Masonry was not regularly conducted in other lodges under the London Grand Lodge? Blaney's Constitutions is not only defective in omitting the list of lodges holding under the London Grand Lodge in 1769, but among the lodges erased he omits many of their numbers and the places of meeting, which is not only annoying, but occasions us much inconvenience. Throughout all the Books of Constitutions we have referred to, as well as Dr. Oliver and Preston's Illustrations, the condition of the Society seems to have depended greatly upon the patronage of royal or noble persons, as Preston remarks above: "The Society at this time seems to have lost much of its consequence," and gives the reason that "the general assemblies and communications not having been honoured with the presence of the nobility."

The next notice we have of the Ancient Masons is under Lord Petre, who succeeded the Duke of Beaufort as Grand Master, May 4, 1772. Preston says: "Many regulations respecting the government of the Fraternity were established during Lord Petre's administration. The meetings of irregular Masons again attracting notice, on the 10th of April, 1777, the following law was enacted: 'That the persons who assemble *in London and elsewhere,* in the character of Masons, calling themselves *Ancient Masons,* and at present said to be under the patronage of the duke of Athol, are not to be countenanced, or acknowledged by any regular lodge, or Mason, under the Constitution of England: nor shall any regular Mason be present at any of their conventions, to give a sanction to their proceedings, under the penalty of forfeiting the privileges of the Society: nor shall any person initiated at any of their irregular meetings be admitted into any lodge without being remade: That this censure shall not extend to any lodge, or Mason, made in Scotland or Ireland, under the constitution of either of these kingdoms; or to any lodge or Mason made abroad, under the patronage of any foreign Grand Lodge in alliance with the Grand Lodge of England; but that such lodge and Mason shall be deemed regular and constitutional.'"

Preston has the following "*Remark.*—This censure only extends to those irregular lodges in London, which seceded from the rest of the fraternity in 1738, and set up an independent government in open defiance of the established authority of the kingdom,

and the general rules of the institution. See pp.
241–244. It *cannot apply to the Grand Lodge in York
city; or to any lodges under that truly ancient and respectable banner*; as the independence and regular proceedings of that assembly have been fully admitted
and authenticated by the Grand Lodge in London, in
the Book of Constitutions printed under their sanction in 1738, p. 196."

Here we have conclusive evidence that the Grand
Lodge at York was existing in 1772, and that it had
lodges working under its " truly ancient and respectable banner." Preston published his " Illustrations
of Masonry" in 1772, and as he had been collecting
matter from the Grand Lodge Records in London
and York, and although the statements in the " Remark " is his writing, it may be considered reliable,
notwithstanding the exception of the York Grand
Lodge is not mentioned in the law enacted, or censured at that Grand Lodge Communication. But the
intelligent reader will at least conceive that the Grand
Lodge went beyond its sphere of authority in mentioning that its *censure shall not extend* to any lodge or
Mason made in Scotland or Ireland with whose
Grand Lodges it was not then in correspondence, or
any foreign Grand Lodge with which it was in alliance; and yet in that same year, 1772, the Duke of
Athol was elected Grand Master of Scotland and
also Grand Master of the Ancients, so called by the
London Masons. Now we believe that the Grand
Lodge of Scotland and the Scottish Masons were as
intelligent and were as well posted in regard to the

condition of Masonry in England, as the Masons in that kingdom themselves; and in electing the Duke of Athol Grand Master, they did it with the full knowledge that they recognized the Grand Lodge and the Masons according to the old Institutions, that is, the Ancient York Masons.

The inconsistency of the above law will thus be apparent, as the Duke of Athol was continued Grand Master of the Ancients, the Ancient York Masons, from 1772 until 1813, when he resigned, for the purpose of promoting the union, in favor of the Duke of Kent, who had been made a Mason under that Constitution. If the Ancients were irregular, then the Grand Master was irregular. He could not consistently be Grand Master of a regular and irregular body of Masons at the same time; *ergo*, all the Masons of Scotland were irregular. We believe that conclusion to be sound and logical. In closing the doors of their Lodges and forbidding Masonic intercourse with the Ancients, the London Masons could not conscientiously recognize their Grand Master, nor any Mason under his jurisdiction. But the *addenda* has a certain signification. Why mention Scotland and Ireland in connection with the York Grand Lodge? No doubt the Masons of those two jurisdictions, through their Grand Masters, bowed reverently and tipt their hats in due acknowledgment of the consideration of being " *deemed regular and constitutional.*"

As the Ancient Masons were not under the jurisdiction of the London Grand Lodge, they were perfectly indifferent to any laws it might pass, and justly too. But the insolence and perversion of truth embodied in the " remark " is beyond comprehension, to assert that the " censure cannot apply to the Grand Lodge in York City," " as the independence and regular proceedings of that assembly have been fully admitted in the Book of Constitutions." In that Book " the old Lodge at York City," meaning the Grand Lodge at York, is charged with " affecting Independency," whilst they concede that " they have the same Constitutions, Charges, Regulations, &c., for substance as their Brethren in England."

We have already quoted the paragraph and commented upon it, but the bold assurance of this later writer has scarcely been equalled in evasive prevarication, in hypocritical pretense, and arrogant assurance in presuming reliance that the readers were so obtuse in intellect and so void of common sense as not to be able to comprehend the common meaning of words. Preston says the independence of the York Grand Lodge was " fully admitted and authenticated," and refers to Anderson, who charges it with *affecting independency*, or rather *ignores the existence of such a body*. The above law and all previous efforts of the London Grand Lodge against those so-called irregular were futile and abortive, and did not affect them, did not cause them to abandon their organization, nor cause them to cease meeting and to make Masons. The reports of the Ancients having seceded from the regular Lodges, so called, constituted by the London Grand Lodge, was a subterfuge to draw attention away from the York Grand Lodge.

It is not only probable, but it may be taken for granted, that many Masons made by the Lodges holding under the London Grand Lodge did leave them and affiliated with York Lodges, hence the many complaints commencing at the organization of the London Grand Lodge, in 1717, down to the time when the arrangements for the union were about completed, in 1813. In the before-mentioned law there is no reference to nor mention made of a new Grand Lodge having been formed. Preston records, that "during his lordship's presidency *some* lodges were erased out of the list for non-conformity to the law, but *many* new ones were added, so that under his banner the Society became truly respectable."

Some erased, and many added, is too indefinite, besides very unsatisfactory. But in all the publications of the Grand Lodge, as well as in Preston, Oliver, Laurie, and some others we will refer to, there is a studied attempt to conceal from the reader all important facts. The statements are all one-sided and mainly following the style of the Reverends Anderson and Desaguliers in evasion of the truth. It would not have answered their purpose to be explicit in their statements, to leave no room for doubt.

What are we to understand by some erased, and many added? Why not state what Lodges were erased? At least, how many of them. There may have been more erased than Lodges added. And as words have meaning, what are we to understand by "the Society became truly respectable" under his Lordship's banner? Does it mean that under former

banners the Society was not respectable? Under
Lord Petre's administration, in May, 1777, commenced
the dispute with the Lodge of Antiquity, of which
Preston was a member. The Grand Lodge, against
every principle of Masonry, interfered with the prerogatives of the Lodge which had, by resolution, resolved on St. John's Day to attend divine service at
St. Dustan's Church in the clothing of the order, and
in addition, the Lodge had "expelled three of its
members for misbehaviour; the Grand Lodge also interfered, and without proper investigation, ordered
them to be reinstated." "With this order the Lodge
refused to comply." The Grand Lodge persisting in
compliance with its "order," the Lodge severed its
connection with the Grand Lodge, notified it of its
separation, "and avowed an alliance *with the Grand
Lodge of all England, held in the city of York*." "The
Grand Lodge, on the other hand, enforced its edicts,
and extended protection to the few (*three*) brethren
whose cause it had espoused, by permitting them to
assemble as a regular lodge, without any warrant,
under the denomination of the Lodge of Antiquity
itself, and suffering them to appear, by their representatives, at the Grand Lodge as the real Lodge of Antiquity, from which they had been excluded, and
which still continued to act by its own immemorial
constitution; anathemas were issued, and several
worthy men expelled the Society for refusing to surrender the property of the Lodge to persons who
had been regularly expelled from it; while printed
letters were circulated with the Grand Treasurer's

accounts, highly derogatory to the dignity of the Society. This produced a schism, which subsisted for the space of ten years."

With the cause of the difficulty between the Grand Lodge and the Lodge of Antiquity we have no concern, but we learn from Preston that the lodge *avowed an alliance with the Grand Lodge at York ;* by this we understand that the Lodge affiliated with the York Grand Lodge, and as it and its members were restored in 1790, the York Grand Lodge was existing at that time. The action of the London Grand Lodge, as stated by Preston, shows an animus in the exercise of power by the Grand Lodge subversive of every principle of Masonry, of Masonic justice and propriety. It was not the first time it took under its wing expelled Masons and gave them authority to work as a Lodge, but in this case of forming a Lodge with the three members expelled from the Lodge of Antiquity, and under that false banner admitting representatives from it to the Grand Lodge, from a Masonic standpoint was so flagrant an act of Masonic wrong to the old Lodge of Antiquity, that we can only conceive that the members of that Lodge, including Preston, must have been devoid of all self-manhood, of the dignity and nobility of the divinely formed human being, of every trait and characteristic of the being created in the likeness of God, and lost to all sense of honor and self-esteem in returning again under the banner of that Grand Lodge guilty of the gross outrages Preston has himself portrayed.

At the Grand Assembly, May 2, 1790, " was confirmed the reinstatement of the members of the Lodge of Antiquity in all their Masonic privileges," and Preston, the author of "Illustrations of Masonry," included. In regard to the *reinstatement* of the Lodge, the causes which produced the result, the preliminary action, consultation, agreement, &c., &c., Preston gives us no information, no light on the subject whatever, no intimation in which body the movement was inaugurated; only the notice of confirmation of reinstatement we have just quoted.

"At the Communication in April, 1782, this important business coming under consideration, after a variety of opinions had been delivered, it was unanimously resolved, that the Grand Master should be requested to adopt such means as his wisdom might suggest, to promote a good understanding among the brethren of the three united kingdoms," (England, Scotland, Ireland.) "Notwithstanding this resolution, the wished-for Union *has not yet been fully accomplished;* but we trust, from some late proceedings in the Grand Lodge of Scotland, through the mediation of the Earl of Moira, that event is not far distant."

"At a meeting of the Grand Lodge in Edinburgh, on the 30th of November, 1803, the Earl of Moira, the acting Grand Master of England, attended, and in an impressive speech related the conduct of the Grand Lodge of England to the irregular Masons of that kingdom, with whom he understood the Grand Lodge of Scotland had established an intercourse. He stated that the hearts and arms of the Grand Lodge which he had the honor to represent, had ever

been open for the reception of the seceding brethren;
but that they had obstinately refused to acknowledge
their error, and return to the bosom of their mother
lodge. He further observed, that though the Grand
Lodge of England *differed in a few trifling observances
from that of Scotland*, the former had ever entertained
for Scottish Masons that affection and regard which
it was the object of Freemasonry to cherish and the
duty of Freemasons to feel."

In this speech of the acting Grand Master of England
we have an admission, publicly made before the Grand
Lodge of Scotland, of a difference *of " a few trifling
observances "* which were unknown to the Scottish
Masons. The admission of the fact is sufficient, coming from such high authority. Of course he would
mention they were *few* and *trifling*, but it was a
necessity to refer to the different observances before
that intelligent body who must have been aware of the
fact; and after mentioning that the differences were few
and trifling, (as he must say something,) he cleverly
turns the subject, expressing "affection and regard"
which the London Grand Lodge "had ever entertained
for Scottish Masons." But the fact must not be lost
sight of that the visit of the acting Grand Master of
the London Grand Lodge to the Grand Lodge of
Scotland was made *twenty-one years* after the Grand
Lodge had "resolved that the Grand Master should
be requested to adopt such means as his wisdom
might suggest to promote a good understanding
among the brethren of the three united kingdoms;"
and *thirty-one years* after the Duke of Athol, Grand

Master elect of Scotland, was chosen Grand Master of the *Ancients*, properly *Ancient York Masons.*

In the interim of the twenty-one years since the adoption of the above resolution, why was no attempt made by the Grand Masters of England to "promote a good understanding with the brethren" of Scotland and Ireland? Was it necessary for the Earl of Moira, the acting Grand Master, to visit the Grand Lodge of Scotland, because the time was propitious, because the Grand Masters had heretofore neglected to carry out that resolution, or because of certain relations with the officials at Edinburgh, that he ventured his visit in expectation to be able to accomplish the object of that resolution so far as Scotland was concerned?

But there may be something in the notice published in the 1738 Book of Constitutions, mentioning Scotland and Ireland as *affecting independency*, to which umbrage was taken, and, as Preston has remarked, "Notwithstanding the pitch of eminence and splendor at which the Grand Lodge in London has arrived, neither the lodges of Scotland nor Ireland court its correspondence."

And as many years had passed since that offensive publication, and the brethren in Scotland and Ireland held no communication with the London Masons, the latter, as a stroke of policy, in the enactment of the law, April 10th, 1777, against the "Ancient Masons" under "the patronage of the Duke of Athol," particularly exempted the Masons in Scotland and Ireland as not including them in the censure, but that they "shall be deemed regular and constitutional," which was no doubt intended both as complimentary and to allay or soften any ill-feelings entertained by the Masons of Scotland and Ireland against the London fraternity, but in our view was an offensive insult to them, as they did not need the recognition of the London Masons to determine their regularity or constitutionality, nor did they court its correspondence.

The speech of the Earl of Moira at Edinburgh, as above quoted, is, if reported correctly, somewhat equivocal. In what view are we to understand, he " related the conduct of the Grand Lodge of England to the irregular Masons "? He could not have referred to any attempt at mediation, of a proposition to appoint committees to discuss questions at issue, to appoint referees; what then was " the conduct of the Grand Lodge "? Overlooking their own deficiencies, they required the Ancient Masons, whose Grand Master was the Duke of Athol, whom they recognized as a regular Mason, to acknowledge that they were irregular Masons, and to submit themselves to the London Grand Lodge, to dissolve their organizations and thus prove to the world not only that they had been in error, but by so doing acknowledge the regularity of the London Grand Lodge. It was to stultify themselves as regular Masons, as Ancient, or Ancient York Masons, and affiliate themselves with the Modern Masons. The *conduct* referred to was prescriptive, not a generous conduct as to an equal whom the Grand Lodge was ready to receive with open hearts and arms. The intent of that speech was to bias the Grand Lodge of Scotland against the Ancient Masons with whose Grand Lodge it was in correspondence, and therefore the salvo of appreciation and regard the London Grand Lodge had always felt towards the Scottish Masons.

"In November, 1801, a charge was presented to the Grand Lodge against *some of its members*, for patronising and *officially* acting as principal officers in an irregular society, calling themselves Ancient Masons, in open violation of the laws of the Grand Lodge. The charge being fully supported, it was determined that the laws should be, enforced against *these offending brethren*, unless they immediately seceded from such irregular meetings. *They* solicited the indulgence of the Grand Lodge for three months, in hopes that during the interval they might be enabled to effect an union of the two Societies. This measure was agreed to; and that no impediment might pervert so desirable an object, the charge against the offending brethren was withdrawn; and a committee, consisting of Lord Moira and several other eminent characters, was appointed to pave the way for the intended union; and every means ordered to be used to bring back the erring Brethren to a sense of their duty and allegiance.

"Lord Moira declared, on accepting his appointment as a member of the Committee, that *he should consider the day on which a coalition was formed, one of the most fortunate in his life;* and that he was empowered by the Prince of Wales to say, his Royal

Highness' arms would ever be open to all the Masons in the kingdom *indiscriminately*.

"On the 9th of February, 1803, it being represented to the Grand Lodge that the irregular Masons still continued refractory, and that, so far from soliciting readmission among the craft, they had not taken any steps to effect an union; their conduct was deemed highly censurable, and the laws of the Grand Lodge were ordered to be enforced against them. It was also 'unanimously resolved, That whenever it shall appear that any Masons under the English Constitution shall in future attend, or countenance, any lodge or meeting of persons, calling themselves *Ancient Masons*, under the sanction of any person claiming the title of Grand Master of England, who shall not have been duly elected in the Grand Lodge, the laws of the Society shall not only be strictly enforced against them, but their names shall be erazed from the list, and transmitted to all the regular lodges under the Constitution of England?"

The following paragraph Oliver has omitted in his Reprint. We copy from Preston, 12th London edition.

"As these censures extend to such a numerous circle, it may for a short time interrupt the general harmony of our meetings; but it is hoped, that when the Brethren of whom the irregular Societies are composed, are aware that, by continuing to assemble without regular sanction, they are acting contrary to the ancient charges of the Order, and encouraging a division in the family of Masons, they will soon reunite under the legal banner, and acknowledge **one** supreme head, to whom all the Fraternity in the kingdom are bound to pay allegiance. Should *any trifling variations in the formalities of the institution* impede the progress of this union, we trust they will be immediately removed, and every Brother vie who shall be most assiduous in preserving the original landmarks of the Order."

Why Oliver should have given an imperfect reprint of Preston in omitting whole paragraphs, is not only suspicious, but a gross deception, as well as a moral and legal wrong. Such conduct is unjustifiable under any circumstances, especially by a minister of the Gospel. " The means justify the end," is an axiom of low politicians, and has been often used as an argument to justify the most heinous atrocities and acts of oppression and deceit in the name of the lowly Jesus, by the clerical profession called to preach his pure ·gospel of peace and good-will.

It was no doubt in the view of the axiom mentioned that Oliver acted. The close of the above paragraph refers to *trifling variations in the formalities,* and Preston does not say on which side these trifling variations had been interpolated. Preston is cautious, but the mere mention of variations in the formalities was sufficient for Oliver to exclude the whole paragraph, as he judged that the Masonic reader knew which side had been guilty of introducing those variations. Now we will look at Preston. The paragraph commences:

" *As these censures extend to such a numerous circle, it may* for a short time *interrupt the general harmony of our meetings;*" which certainly is an admission that there were many of the Masons of the so-called regular lodges inclined favorably towards the Ancient Masons, because the latter quotations commence with a charge against "some of the members" of the London Grand Lodge, and it could only be the members in its jurisdiction which could "interrupt the general harmony of *our* (the London Grand Lodge) meetings."

Neither Preston nor the London Grand Lodge would admit that the Ancient Masons comprised a *numerous* circle. There is nothing in the other portions of the paragraph omitted by Oliver which will not apply solely and directly to the London Grand Lodge and the Masons under its Constitution. Who were the first to make a division among the Masons of England? The London Masons. They formed a Grand Lodge in 1717, and in doing so, acted "contrary to the ancient charges of the order," and that certainly was "encouraging a division in the family of Masons."

It would seem as if the whole paragraph was covertly intended by Preston to apply to the London Grand Lodge and its constituents. The action of the London Grand Lodge was altogether in reference and applicable only to its own members. A charge was brought against *some* of its members — it may have been two, twenty, a hundred or more, sufficient however to cause much annoyance to the Grand Lodge — and resulted in the passage of a stringent resolution, quoted above, as a caution to its own membership. The matter of a three months' delay and the preparations for a union may have been so, although it appears to us to have been interpolated. The subject is then changed from its own members to the oft-repeated *irregular Masons*, against whom "the laws of the Grand Lodge were ordered to be enforced," from which we infer that the uncertain "some of its members" went over to the Ancient York members.

The declaration of Lord Moira, "that he should consider the day on which a coalition was formed one of the most fortunate in his life," and that of the Prince of Wales, his "arms would ever be open to all the Masons in the kingdom indiscriminately," shows the anxiety of the highest officers of the London Grand Lodge to form a union with the Ancient Masons, even without them conceding any claim of superiority and on terms of perfect equality, as regular Masons made in regularly constituted Masonic bodies, notwithstanding the fuss and bluster of secession, irregular Masons, &c., of Grand Lodge enactments.

"On the 12th of February, 1806, the Earl of Moira in the chair, informed the Grand Lodge, that during his residence in Edinburgh he had visited the Grand Lodge of Scotland, and taken the opportunity of explaining to it *the extent and importance of this Grand Lodge*, and also the *origin and situation* of those Masons in England who meet under the authority of the Duke of Athol; that the brethren of the Grand Lodge of Scotland had *expressed themselves till then greatly misinformed of those circumstances*, having been always led to think that *this Society was of a very recent date*, and of no magnitude; but being more thoroughly convinced of their error, they were desirous that the strictest union and most intimate communication should subsist between this Grand Lodge and the Grand Lodge of Scotland; and as the first step towards so important an object, and in testimony of the wishes of the Scots Masons, his Royal Highness, the Prince of Wales, had been unanimously elected Grand Master of Scotland."

[Without closing our quotation, we remark on the above, that the Earl of Moira was the Commander-in-Chief of his Majesty's forces in Scotland, and *acting* Grand Master of the Grand Lodge of England under the Prince of Wales, who was Grand Master. The high position of the Earl, and consequent influence, caused his *ex parte* statements, made in 1803, to deeply impress the Scots Masons with a desire to be instrumental in effecting a union between the two divisions of the Masons in England. The Earl's statements were evidently taken with some caution, notwithstanding the Earl's remarks that they "expressed themselves till then greatly misinformed," which we believe they did not express, but were interpolated by him, as it was not until 1806 that the Grand Lodge of Scotland expressed the desire that the strictest union may subsist between the Grand Lodge of England and the Grand Lodge of Scotland; and as the first step to that important object they elected the Grand Master of England, the Prince of Wales, the Grand Master of the Grand Lodge of Scotland. What the Earl's reply was to the observation made by the Grand Lodge of Scotland, that they always thought that the London Grand Lodge "was of a very recent date," he does not tell.   Did he go back to Athelstane, 926 to 1567, or to the revolution in 1717, and mention the true circumstances of the formation of the London Grand Lodge?   We doubt that the thought "of a very recent date" was expressed, but if it was it must have brought the color to his cheeks, as he could not answer truly, and must have evaded any reference to the origin of the Society, the London Grand Lodge.   We now continue the quotation from Preston.]

"The Grand Master in the chair further informed the Grand Lodge, that the Grand Lodge of Scotland had expressed its *concern that any difference should subsist amongst the Masons of England, and that the lodges meeting under the sanction of the Duke of Athol should have withdrawn themselves from the protection of the Ancient Grand Lodge of England*, but hoped that measures might be adopted to produce a reconciliation, and that the lodges now holding irregular meetings would return to their duty and again be received into the bosom of the Fraternity.   That in reply his Lordship had stated his firm belief that this Grand Lodge would readily *concur in any measures* that might be proposed for establishing union and harmony amongst the general body of Masons; but that after the rejection of the propositions made by this Grand Lodge three years ago, it could not now,

consistent with its honor or the dignity of its illustrious Grand Master, make any further advances; but
that as it still retained its disposition to promote the
general interest of the Craft, it would always be open
to accept of the *mediation* of the Grand Lodge of
Scotland, if it should think proper to interfere on the
subject.   Whereupon it was resolved, that a letter be
written to the Grand Lodge of Scotland, expressive
of the desire of this Grand Lodge, that the strictest
union may subsist between the Grand Lodge of England and the Grand Lodge of Scotland; and for that
purpose, that the actual Masters and Wardens of the
lodges under the authority of the Grand Lodge of
Scotland who may be in London, on producing proper testimonials, shall have a seat in this Grand
Lodge, and be permitted to vote on all occasions."

In this portion of the paragraph it will be seen that
the Grand Lodge of Scotland˙ expresses a concern
that any *difference should subsist among the Masons of
England;* that surely was a matter of regret as well
of concern, and the concern is continued "that the
lodges meeting under the sanction of the Duke of
Athol should have *withdrawn* themselves from the
protection of the *ancient Grand Lodge of England.*"

We believe that here is a clear intimation that the
Earl of Moira practised a deception in his statements
to the Grand Lodge of Scotland.   The Grand Lodge
of England that he represented was not an ancient
Grand Lodge in any sense; it did not consider itself
as ancient; the term never was applied to it in any
of its publications, its correspondence, its transac-

tions, or its expressions on any occasion whatever, unless the Earl in his statements to the Scots Masons represented that his Grand Lodge had an existence prior to 1717.

The term ancient, as applied by the Grand Lodge of Scotland, would prove that a deception was practised in applying it to the body from which the lodges under the Duke of Athol had withdrawn. The word ancient was originally applied to the York Masons, as, *Ancient York Masons;* the London Masons, after forming an independent Grand Lodge, changed the secret work of the Order, on account of which many of its members went and attached themselves to the York Masons; and as the London Grand Lodge pronounced them "seceders," "irregular Masons," &c., they in return called the others *Modern Masons,* as they had infringed upon the ancient charges and usages, and stated that as they had not made any changes in the body of Masonry, but maintained the ancient customs and ceremonials, they were the only ancient Masons.

Because the Masons under the 1717 organization were pronounced Modern, they applied the term "ancient," "irregular," &c., to the others, but never mentioned them in connection with York Masons; the York Masons were completely tabooed by them, as if there were no such body of Masons.

The hope expressed by the Grand Lodge of Scotland "that measures would be adopted to produce a reconciliation," opened the way for the Earl of Moira "to accept the mediation of the Grand Lodge of

Scotland, if it should think proper to interfere on the subject." Upon the Earl's statement the Grand Lodge resolved, that a letter be written to the Grand Lodge of Scotland expressive of its desire that the strictest union may subsist between the two Grand Lodges, and conceding to the actual Masters and Wardens of the lodges in Scotland when in London a seat in the Grand Lodge and the privilege of voting on all occasions.

In all these representations of the Earl of Moira, there is an evident design of misrepresentation and deception towards his own Grand Lodge, as well as the Grand Lodge of Scotland. His statement to his own Grand Lodge, 1806, made more than two years after he visited the Grand Lodge of Scotland, is considerably embellished with observations that do not appear to have been made before the Grand Lodge of Scotland. The explaining "the extent and importance of this (the London) Grand Lodge, and also the origin and situation of those Masons in England who meet under the authority of the Duke of Athol," he could not do without departing from truth. It would be most interesting to know the nature of the explanations, if any such were made. The *extent* and *importance* of his Grand Lodge he might magnify as much as he pleased before a Hindoo audience unacquainted with the language as well as the existent facts; but before a body of Scots Masons, noted for their intelligence and general characteristic of examining, investigating, and informing themselves on every subject in which they are interested, is too big a plum to swallow, and mentioning "that the members of the Grand Lodge of Scotland expressed themselves till then greatly misinformed," as if none of them had any knowledge of Preston's illustrations, which had been published a third of a century before, and run through many editions, and was as well known in Scotland as in England.

Lawrie, in his History of Freemasonry, 1804 ed., mentions the Earl of Moira being at the meeting of the Grand Lodge, November, 1803, and reports almost substantially the same words as having been spoken by him as in our quotation from Preston. Lawrie has *Ancient* Masons, and Preston *irregular* Masons. The Earl of Moira certainly did not tell the truth in saying that the Grand Lodge of Scotland expressed the desire "that the strictest union and most intimate communication should subsist between this Grand Lodge and the Grand Lodge of Scotland." If the Earl of Moira as quoted made the statement to his Grand Lodge, then he deceived it, as at that meeting his Grand Lodge, after his statement, "Resolved, that a letter be written to the Grand Lodge of Scotland expressive of its desire that the strictest union may subsist between the two Grand Lodges;" which initiated a movement for the union and fraternal correspondence between the two Grand Lodges.

"On the 12th April, 1809, it was resolved, That this Grand Lodge do agree in opinion with the committee of charity; that it is not necessary any longer to continue in force those measures which were resorted to in or about the year.1739, respecting *irreg-*

ular Masons, and do therefore *enjoin* the several lodges *to revert to the ancient landmarks of the Society.*" This concludes our review of Preston, 12th London ed., which brings the work down to the close of 1811. Oliver has the following significant information added in his Reprint of Preston to the above paragraph: "This measure was carried into effect by the appointment (with the sanction of the Grand Master) of an occasional lodge named 'The Lodge of Promulgation,' which will appear to have been a step preparatory to the so much desired union of Masons Ancient and Modern."

It is conclusive from the above action of the committee of charity, and the concurrence of the Grand Lodge, that it was necessary, preparatory to a union, for them *to return again to the ancient usages*, to no longer continue the innovations or changes made in the ceremonial, which was the cause of so many of its members leaving it and affiliating with the Ancient Masons; "to revert again to the ancient landmarks of the Society." Hence the *Lodge of Promulgation* was appointed to instruct the Masons under the London Grand Lodge what the ancient landmarks were, and to no longer use the ceremonials substituted in 1739; and hence at the union there was so little difference found between the Masons under the two Grand Lodges by the Lodge of Reconciliation through its committees of examination. The course adopted was a clear admission on the part of the London Grand Lodge that it had departed from the ancient landmarks, and as a consequence, that it was the cause of continued secession from its ranks, and by logical deduction they were the irregular Masons and not the ancients, and therefore they were justly entitled to the offensive appellation of "Modern Masons."

Prior to the articles of union, Oliver has the following: "When by the accession of the Prince of Wales to the Regency of the United Kingdom, etiquette seemed to require his resignation as Grand Master, the Duke of Sussex was, by the unanimous acclamation of the Grand Lodge, elected to fill that high and important situation; and the Prince Regent soon after graciously condescended to accept the title of Grand Patron of the Order.

"It was early discovered, that the Duke of Sussex's whole heart was bent on accomplishing that great *desideratum* of Masons, the union of the two Fraternities who had been mistermed *Ancient* and *Modern;* and his high station in life certainly carried with it an influence which could not have been found in an humbler individual.

"It has been already said, that his Grace the Duke of Athol was at the head of the Ancient Fraternity — for, to be explicit without circumlocution, we must at present make use of these terms relatively. The fact is, that the Ancients after their secessions continued to hold their meetings without acknowledging a superior, till 1772; when they chose for their Grand Master the Duke of Athol, who was then Grand Master elect for Scotland.

"This venerable nobleman, *we may presume*, was

convinced by the Royal Duke's arguments, strength-
ened by his own good sense and benevolent mind,
how desirable must be an actual and cordial union of
the two societies under one head; because, to pave
the way for the measure, his Grace, in the handsomest
manner, shortly after resigned his seat of Grand Master, recommending his Royal Highness the Duke of
Kent (who had been made a Mason under that constitution) as his successor; who was accordingly
elected and installed Grand Master of that body of
Masons, at Willis's Rooms, St. James' Square, on the
1st of December, 1813, on which occasion his Royal
Highness most liberally professed, that he had accepted the office with the sole view of coöperating,
more effectually, perhaps, with his Illustrious Brother
of Sussex, in promoting and cementing the so much
desired union."

From the foregoing extracts, and our review of
them, the reader must be satisfied that the several
Books of Constitution authorized by the London
Grand Lodge were written with the object of lauding
its own organization, magnifying its own importance
in the estimation of its readers, pandering to a considerable extent to the nobility, and omitting such
important events and occurrences which they deemed
prejudicial to them as the leading and governing
body of Masons, and considered all others as irregular who worked not under their banner, did not
worship at their altars.

The history of Anderson, published in the 1723
edition, is in the main copied in future editions, which

as an ecclesiastic work may be read with interest by
certain classes of religionists, but to intelligent Freemasons it is of no account, possesses no value, and
as a contribution to literature, with the exception of
its myths and fables, is a compilation full of errors
and misstatements, which any intelligent schoolboy of
to-day would be ashamed to acknowledge himself the
author of.

The Ancient Charges in the 1723 and 1738 editions are different, and one or the other must be corrupted, as we will show, and which in our opinion
was the case with both, and indeed all which are accepted at the present day as the *Simon pure* Ancient
Charges.

The Proceedings of the Grand Lodge from the
1738 publication down to the union in 1813, give us
little information as to the business brought before
the Grand Lodge; the abstracts are most meagre, relating chiefly to Elections of Grand Masters, Installa-
tions and Ceremonials, Feasts, Laying of Corner-
Stones, references to irregular Masons and Seceders.
As among a quantity of chaff a few grains of
wheat will be found, so the investigating student
who will carefully wade through the pages of these
volumes will find here and there some remark, some
statement, which he can appropriate in some line of
thought.

It will be noticed by the above extracts from
Oliver, and all preceding action of the London
Grand Lodge in reference to a union, the great de-
sire for that desideratum was on its part, and not on

the side of the Ancients, and perhaps that would not have been attained in this century, if at all, had it not been for a concatenation of circumstances favorable to the Grand Lodge in the attainment of its long-sought desire. The influences of the eminent and leading minds of the Grand Lodge were brought to bear upon the Grand Master, the Duke of Athol, who seconded their truly worthy, beneficent Masonic design, which ultimated in the union of two bands of Brother Masons who had for many years been estranged from each other.

It would appear, from the liberal remark made by His Royal Highness the Prince of Wales, " that his arms would ever be open to *all the Masons in the kingdom indiscriminately*," that his wisdom and conciliatory influence, more than aught else, were promotive of producing that very happy result.

The enactments of the Grand Lodge against the irregular Masons produced no result ; they were ineffective, and would lead to the belief that the Ancient Masons were a strong body, capable of supporting and maintaining their organization in defiance of every effort of the self-styled regular Masons.

As the Union was in prospect by the resignation of the Duke of Athol, and recommending the Duke of Kent as his successor, who was elected Grand Master, with the understanding that he could better coöperate with the Prince Regent in bringing about a union between the two bodies of Masons, the offensive terms, Seceders, irregular Masons, were not used, and the distinctive appellations, Ancient and Modern,

were discarded.   In the arrangement of the articles
of Union, and the celebration of the event, there was
no distinction made : all were equal according to their
position and attainments, and all had to submit to the
ceremonials, usages, etc., that both through their
committees had agreed upon were the Ancient Landmarks, and all had to go through the process of re-
obligation.

As in preceding remarks we stated that the organization of the Grand Lodge in 1717 was not a revival
but a revolution, we now quote Lawrie, although he
takes Anderson's statement of there only being four
Lodges in London at that time.   "Four Lodges only
existed in the South, and few hopes could be entertained of a revival while the seat of the Grand Lodge
was at such a distance as the city of York.   In such
circumstances the four Lodges met in 1717, and in
order to give vigor to their declining cause and advance the interests of the fraternity in the South, they
elected themselves into a Grand Lodge, and chose An-
thony Sayer, Esq., for their *first Grand Master*."

" The motive which suggested this institution was
certainly laudable and useful ; but every person must be
aware *that the four Lodges were guilty of a considerable
impropriety* in omitting to request the countenance of
the Grand Lodge of York."   Lawrie countenanced
the London Grand Lodge, and in relation to the ancients he adopted Preston's views, but in the above
candid remarks he wrote in favor of truth, of Masonic usage, as an intelligent, enlightened Mason.

Lawrie continues : " Notwithstanding this negligence, the greatest harmony subsisted between the two Grand Lodges till 1734." The word *negligence* is certainly a mild term to apply to seditious conduct, especially as he acknowledges the existence of the Grand Lodge of York.

In that year, 1734, however, Lawrie says: "The Grand Lodge of England having granted constitutions to Lodges within the District of York, without the consent of their Grand Lodge, incurred to such a degree the displeasure of the York Masons that the friendly intercourse" was completely broken off. Also: "In 1739, some trifling innovations upon the ancient customs of the order having been imprudently sanctioned by the Grand Lodge of England, *several* of the old London Masons were highly offended, and after *seceding* from the Grand Lodge and *pretending* to act under the York constitution, they gave themselves the appellation of Ancient Masons," and called the others modern. And further on, Lawrie says: "The Moderns undoubtedly departed from their *usual caution and propriety* of conduct by authorizing the slightest innovations upon the ceremonies of an ancient institution." Although Lawrie censures also the Ancients, yet he writes altogether in the interest of the London Masons.

In criticizing the above remarks, copied after Preston, it is not reasonable to believe that the seceding of *several old London Masons* could have given the Grand Lodge such unrest as to consume the time of its meetings for a long period. "Several" is not so indefinite as to embrace hundreds or fifty ; it

means a·small number; there were sufficient, however, to act under the York constitution and assume a
distinct title, even according to the author. We have
only the authority of partisan antagonist writers in
reference to statements relating to the Masons not
under the London Grand Lodge.

Anderson does not mention the Ancient Masons
as he published in 1738. Preston mentions them, as
Lawrie, in 1739; but Entick first refers to them in
1755, sixteen years after Preston. Now we hold that
the word York was intentionally omitted in calling
them Ancient Masons, in order to make it appear
that the Ancients were a new organization of seceders
from the London Grand Lodge. Therefore the assertion, *pretending* to act under the York constitution.
Why should they *pretend?* and why simply assume
the name of *ancient* only, if they acted under the York
constitution? It would seem conclusive that Ancient
York Masons was the correct appellation, as it is a
title handed down to this time, has always been in
use in applying it to the York Masons, and Ancient
Masons has no particular significance; besides, the
York Masons were completely *tabooed* by the London
Masons, for which reason the word *ancient* only is applied to those who seceded from them and acted under the York constitution.

It must not be forgotten that we have only Preston
as authority for the statement that those who acted
under the York constitution assumed the name Ancient Masons. There is no other authority until 1755,
when Entick, near the close of the Grand Lodge trans-

actions, applies it. But Preston mentions them as professing that "the *ancient tenets and practices of Masonry* were preserved by them," and that the *new* Grand Lodge which they instituted was "professedly on the *ancient* system." What was that ancient system? the tenets and practices of Masonry which were preserved by them, if not the Ancient York system which they as Masons originally received from the Mother Grand Lodge at York? From the foregoing reviews there can be no doubt whatever that Ancient York Masons was the real appellation, and that the " new Grand Lodge " was a District, or limited Grand Lodge, appointed by the York Grand Lodge, with defined powers, within London and its vicinity. It could hardly be expected that any writer, a Mason under and a member of the London Grand Lodge, would stultify his Grand Lodge by the publication of facts as they existed which the Grand Lodge itself by every possible means aimed to keep out of view, with the object to have it believed that the Grand Lodge at York was no longer in existence. That such is the truth, its own publications prove, and every advantage was taken of the fact that the Grand Lodge at York never published anything; and this is additional evidence that the so-called Ancient Masons were Ancient York Masons, as they never published any of their transactions, in accordance, no doubt, with positive rules governing the Grand Lodge, save the *Ahiman Rezons* published by Lawrence Dermott.

No history of Freemasonry of the past and present century has been truly written, because of the myths and fables that were incorporated with legitimate facts by the early writers, particularly the Reverends Anderson and Desaguliers, whose Books of Constitutions have been not only received as standard authorities, but their versions have been accepted by the generality of subsequent writers and readers in the whole of their contents as established truths.

A writer of history, in order to be truthful to himself and to the public, ought to examine carefully every statement, and not accept as true, come from what source it may, without an exhaustive investigation of the subject. The investigation should be free from all bias of preconceived opinions, of educational teachings, of traditional authorities, of prejudices of any kind whatever. In regard to the subject under consideration, it should always be had in view that the information we have is mainly one-sided and tinged with every shade of prejudice, of hostile animus that a revolutionary body could bring to bear in claim of sovereignty and absolute dominion.

The London Grand Lodge formed in 1717, not satisfied with continued aggressions upon the rights of the Grand Lodge at York from 1567 to its ultimate act in severing its ties from its parent Grand Lodge and establishing an independent Masonic government, but claimed to be the only Masonic authority in England. In the exercise of that claim it set at defiance all Masonic law, Masonic comity, Masonic justice, and not only violated the *essentia* of the obligation to which every member and all Masons are covenanted, but justified itself in innovating upon the

ancient charges and secret teachings of the institution. The London Grand Lodge was not a legitimate body of Masons; it had no regular Masonic
existence, nor were the persons made Masons under
its constitutions perfect and regular Masons; they all
of them had to undergo the process of healing, of
being properly instructed, of being reobligated at the
union in 1813, as well as the Ancient York Masons
with whom they united in forming the present Grand
Lodge of England.

The history preceding the union and the articles
agreed upon, as well as the arrangements prior to in
appointing a Lodge of Promulgation, all conclusively
prove that the union was a necessity to establish the
regular Masonic status of the London·Masons, and
such we believe was the view taken by the Prince
Regent, the Grand Patron of Masons, in promoting
the union and making the statement that his arms
would always be open to all the Masons in the
kingdom indiscriminately.

The early authorized publications of the London
Masons, Anderson's, Entick's, Blaney's, and Nor-
thouk's Books of Constitutions, were not written in
the cause of Truth, nor were the various Freemason's
Companions, which were mainly copies so far as the
transactions of the Grand Lodge were printed, and
they all express more in what is omitted than what is
related. Dr. Oliver, who is by no means reliable in
his Reprint of Preston, commenced where Preston
left off immediately preceding the union, and continued his History down to 1842; but in no part of

his work does he comment upon the causes which
led to union, nor the preparations prior to, neither the
arrangements and articles agreed upon for the consummation of that desirable event, although much
might be said on these subjects.

As we have confined ourselves to the periods
between 1567 and 1813, when the regular Grand
Lodge of England was formed, a review of the proceedings had in relation to and at the union is beyond the limits and scope of our intended publication.

During the past one hundred and fifty years, no
writers, until within a decade, have attempted a
critical examination of the authorized versions of
Freemasonry, although scarce a page of them will
bear the scrutiny of enlightened investigation; and
strange as it may appear even at this day, in this age
of intellectual progress so prolific of Masonic publications emanating from Masonic Grand Bodies, Peri-
odicals, Books, &c., all written with the view of pro-
mulgating Masonic knowledge, yet the brains are
mainly exercised in commenting upon, expounding
and elaborating the various subjects all in the same
vein of thought, without analysis, research, or investigation out of a common beaten track.

Brother Findel of Leipzig, and other European
writers, have in recent years, in a highly commendable spirit, with fervency and zeal, entered upon a
course of investigation, to satisfy themselves of the
truth of historical statements published in the Books
of Constitutions, by searching the records to ascertain if such documents existed or emanated from the

source to which they referred; and although we dis-
agree with them in many essentials, as our review
shows, to the conclusions they arrived at in relation
to the early history of Masonry in England, and the
Ancient Grand Lodge at York, and the so-called
Ancient Masons, yet their researches have disclosed
much information, interesting, valuable, and important, to the Masonic student, and for which, and
for carrying their investigations outside of the popular trodden paths, they are entitled to the thanks of
the whole fraternity of Masons, and will be ap-
preciated in the future for their indefatigable efforts
in the cause of consistency and Truth.

As our writing extends only to the Union of the
two Masonic bodies in England, in 1813, and the
organization of the present Grand Lodge of England, we deem it proper to briefly state here that the
Union was not only an event much to be desired and
coveted, but the conduct and management was highly
honorable and creditable to both fraternities; and the
United Grand Lodge since that time has maintained
its integrity as a conservator of Masonic principles, and
in carrying out the aims of Masonry in its benevolent institutions and charities. Our preceding remarks, therefore, in regard to the London Masons
and London Grand Lodge, cannot in any sense apply
to the Masons of England since the union, nor to
the United Grand Lodge of England.

We now resume our review and turn to Anderson
1723 ed. "The Charges of a Freemason extracted
from the ancient records of Lodges beyond Sea, and

of those in England, Scotland, and Ireland, for the
use of the Lodges in London." It would be an idle‘
and indeed a silly question to ask an intelligent
Mason where the records are to be found from which
were extracted the Charges of a Freemason. Where
were those lodges located? If the Charges formed
the basis of instruction to *new-made Brethren* in Ireland, Scotland, England, and beyond Sea, they must
have been known to the London Masons. But they
were extracted from a *variety* of Ancient Records.
Then the records were not uniform, and Masons in
different parts were instructed differently, and in order
to make the extracts from the records of Lodges, Anderson must have had access to the records which he
could only have had by visiting the lodges, and could
definitely have stated where the records were, but he
does not tell. He mentions *England*. *London is in
England ;* and according to his statement, *four lodges
and "some old Brothers"* met and formed a Grand
Lodge in London in 1717. Had those four lodges
no records, no uniform mode of instructing new-made
Masons? If they had a uniform mode, why search
the records of lodges beyond sea, Scotland and Ireland? Was it to form a new code of Charges? We
believe that the entire code of Ancient Charges was
the production of Desaguliers and Anderson, and
that there is no truth in their being extracted from
any records outside of London. But Anderson
cannot be believed, he stultifies, contradicts himself,
ol which the following is proof. In his remarks,
1738 edition, following the dedication "The *Author*

to the Reader," he reports : " The Free-Masons *had always* a Book in *Manuscript* call'd the *Book* of *Constitutions*, (of which they have several very ancient Copies remaining,) containing not only their *Charges* and *Regulations ;* but also the History of *Architecture* from the Beginning of Time," &c. " But they had no *Book* of *Constitutions* in Print, till his *Grace* the present Duke of *Montagu*, when *Grand Master*, ordered *me to peruse* the old *Manuscripts*, and digest *the Constitutions* with a just *Chronology*."

If Anderson, 1738 ed., as well as the 1723 ed., and subsequent writers are to be believed, Masonic Lodges existed centuries in England before the 1723 Ancient Charges were published, and it cannot be believed that in all those years the lodges had no uniform mode of instruction, at least approximately so. It would exceed our limits to enter into a review of the several Charges, although a critical examination will show many points of inconsistency blended in with sound morals and wholesome advice. But Anderson in 1738 is not the Anderson of 1723. He must have swung around another circle, have gone another voyage beyond sea, have visited other lodges and extracted from other records, as his code of Charges in 1738 *differ* in material points from his 1723 code. As the two different Ancient Charges have been before the fraternity at least one hundred and thirty odd years, and Anderson claims the authorship of both, and as the fraternity swear by Anderson, it seems somewhat strange that in all these years no attempt has been made to investigate and ascertain

the reason why Anderson in 1738, with the approval
of the Grand Lodge, altered the Charges approved in
1723. We called attention to the fact so far back as
1855, while reprinting Dermott's *Ahiman Rezon*, and
after a careful examination at the time, we came to
the conclusion that the changes were made to ap-
proximate more nearly to the teachings of the York
Masons, as about that period, say from 1734 to 1739,
there was much dissatisfaction among the London
Masons, and many went over and joined the York
Lodges, which induced Anderson to make the
changes in his Book of 1738 Constitutions. Since
we first called the attention of the craft to the said
changes in the Charges, a few writers, in referring to
the subject, made no other comments than to remark
that the differences were unimportant or of a trifling
nature. To make a difference in a fundamental law
to alter the Ancient Landmarks, is by no means a
trifling or unimportant matter; it is a great wrong,
an offence criminal in the highest degree. But the
importance or unimportance of the differences is not
what is wanted to be known, therefore all remarks in
that direction are irrelevant and an evasion of a
question of the highest importance — the cause or
reason *why* the changes were made? But the differences in the two codes of Ancient Charges are by no
means trifling or unimportant, and although we have
stated that we could not review the several Charges,
as our space was limited, we will notwithstanding
give a brief space to the first of the Charges. In the
1723 ed., the Masons in Ancient times " were charged

in every Country *to be of the Religion of that Country.*"
In the 1738 ed., St. Paul's mode was adopted, and they
were only charged to *comply with the usages* of each
country. The difference between the two is wide,
and to say that *to be obliged to change one's religion,* or
to simply comply with the usages, is an unimportant
difference, is an abuse of language, an insult to common sense.

Anderson was the first to introduce sectarian ideas
into the fundamental principles, the Ancient Charges,
as we have shown; and confining ourselves to the
first, under the head, " Concerning God and Religion,"
we ask, Why mention religion ?   An erroneous opinion is very generally held as to the meaning of that
word.   In writing and conversation it is used as a
substitute for *creed,* as the Catholic, Protestant, Pres-
byterian, Baptist religion, and in a more general sense,
as the Jewish, Christian, Mohammedan religion.   But
that cannot be the true sense and meaning of the
word religion.   It is a common remark of those who
hold liberal views, those who are not creed-bound,
that there is only one true religion, which approxi-
mates more nearly to our view.   We hold religion to
be an active principle of the soul common to humanity, and manifested in every human being according to his or her conscious perceptions.   That is
religion only which the active principle exhibits in
kindly, beneficent acts, in doing good in any sense
by demonstrative manifestation, and in useful employment, whatever the occupation may be.   It is in no sense
passive, and cannot be, because it is a divine element,

partaking of the essence and spirit of its divine Original. God is never at rest. Incessantly[7] and eternally
God is omnipresent throughout the infinite universe,
and throughout illimitable space there is no single
spot in which the Almighty hands are at rest, in which
the greatest worker of us all is not ever and unceas-
ingly actively manifested. Religion is the divine vitalizing element in humanity which promotes the
world's civilization, the world's progress in enlightenment, in the improvement in the arts, in science, in
humanizing efforts to elevate and advance the race,
to conduce to the comfort and happiness of mankind.
Creedal systems, or so-called religion, are the manifestations of cold intellectual efforts ; they are not
outwrought of the divine vitalizing element, are not
instrumental in promoting peace and good will, but
have always been the *great disturbing element in the
world*, exciting animosity, hatred, and strife among
men, opposing all improvement of the race in knowledge and scientific development, and retarding the
progress of mankind to *higher planes of moral and
spiritual life*.

Although the first charge has the caption, " Concerning God and Religion," yet God is not mentioned
in the entire charge; there is no reference whatever to
God in any sense, an omission certainly singular in
consideration of the title. The charge commences :
"A Mason is obliged by his Tenure to obey the moral
law." In what sense are we to understand that different from the obligation of universal humanity to
live up to their highest conscientious convictions ?

To obey the divine commands is obligatory upon all men, a solemn duty due from the creature to the Creator. The charge, therefore, is simply superfluous verbiage. But if "by his Tenure," that is, holding a relation to the fraternity, Anderson intended to make it appear because of that relation Masons did more strictly " obey the moral law " than those who were not Masons, then he should have given some evidence of the truth palpable to public observation. He could not mean that Masons had a higher code of ethics than was known to the outside world; that would conflict with the Creed of the Church of which he was a minister. The above quoted sentence continues : "And if he rightly understands the Art, he will never be a stupid Atheist nor an irreligious Libertine " What is the difference between a believing and non-believing, an irreligious and religious libertine ? The charge implies a difference distinguishing an irreligious from a religious libertine. If a Mason rightly understands the Art, that is, the mysteries of Masonry, he will never be a *stupid* Atheist nor an irreligious libertine. There are many persons who believe there are none who are not believers in a creative intelligence; that there are no Atheists in the sense generally applied, but that all human beings are Theists, and acknowledge the existence of God, each according to his or her understanding. It is mainly the inconsistent views held of the attributes, the power and its exercise, and the original design of a prescient God, that scepticism is so prevalent; and because sceptics cannot accept the views entertained by teachers of creedal systems, they are considered Atheists or infidels, without regard to their moral principles, or the truly divine life they may lead in useful employment, in beneficent efforts in relieving suffering humanity.

We might largely extend our criticism on the first charge as to the " expedient only to oblige Masons to that religion in which all men agree, leaving their particular opinions to themselves," which simply means nothing at all, because there is no religion in which all men agree, and in reference to God there is the greatest confusion of ideas, no possible approximation to a unity of opinion or belief, and saint and sage, cramped by ancient authority, are equally, if not more, beclouded than the " poor Indian whose untutored mind sees God in clouds and hears him in the wind."

The Materialists do not believe in a God as represented to them, but they believe there is an intelligent power behind moving the machinery of the universe and unfolding material phenomena ; and that is as clear as the most learned divine can describe the Universal Father. Moreover, the Materialist acknowledges that intelligent, invisible power is beyond human ken or reason. Can infallible Pope or fallible teacher of the Word more clearly tell what God is ? The Materialist considers it incumbent upon him to live in obedience to the laws of nature in order to enjoy this life properly, and regards that he has duties towards his fellow-beings, therefore he must be just, honest, and live a life of rectitude. Is not that obeying the moral law? The Materialist neither believes nor denies the existence of conscious life after what is called death, after the mortal body is entombed. That view differs very little from that of religionists generally. If the soul is entombed and lies dormant until *the end of things*, or "judgment day," so called, it might as well be annihilated. The popular religionists do not believe in the continued conscious existence of the soul, but will have a "millennium" at least, in a far future that will never be. In our view the soul is not buried with the physical body. It can never die, never lose its conscious life, nor can its consciousness be in abeyance for a single moment. Conscious life is not in flesh, blood, nor muscle, neither in nerve, system, nor brain.

We hold that progress in spirit - life is eternal. That according to our conscious perceptions we are ever attracted towards God, the aspirations of the soul ever drawn upward to the Infinite. We live and move and have our being, and ever will, through the eternal ages, in the divine Being. In the economy of God's government we each have a distinct individuality; that individuality cannot be destroyed, but ever and ever will unfold in wisdom and love approximating more nearly to the unattainable Infinite. We believe that often and more frequently than is believed that in the dying state the visible presence of loved ones passed away is recognized, and glimpses of spirit-life are visible; and further, that if we all lived more in obedience to the laws of nature, the laws of God, the veil that hides from our view the invisible world would gradually become transparent. There is so much doubt in regard to the future in the theologies of the world, so much inconsistency in theologic teachings, that unless we divest ourselves of all that kind of authoritative indoc· trination, we cannot have a consistent knowledge of God, of the attributes of divine Being, nor of our relations to the source and fount of all life. Hence the diversity of so-called religions, and the absurdity of Anderson and Masonic teachers of the present day talking about "that religion in which all men agree," which, if referring to a qualification of "a belief in God," then, as shown above, universal humanity, the Materialist, Atheist, Infidel, all believe in an invisible power or force demonstrated throughout the universe, and that is all that can ever be known of God by Pope, priest, or finite being.

If we are to understand Anderson that a simple "belief in God" constitutes religion, then there can be no need of creeds, there would be no different systems of faith, there would be throughout the world but one religion. The only considerations of belief would then be some universal standard, what God is, the nature and attributes of that Being which mankind would accept. But the mere belief in God amounts to nothing. There is too much involved in the inquiry to accept a simple affirmative assent. Something ought to be known about that belief, its nature, character, as there should be some foundation for a belief as a basis that the conscious perceptions accept and appropriate as true. Religion, in its true acceptance, is *the visible manifestation of God outwrought in uses to humanity.* Religion is not manifested in sun, moon, nor stars, neither in tree, bud, flower, nor animal, but God is in all material phenomena throughout the universe. In and through these phenomena God's religion is made visible to universal humanity, in the prescient wisdom of *providing the needs of all created beings.* Thus true religion, God's religion, is manifest to mankind, and through the physical senses is illustrated what true religion is, and its mode of manifestation, in considering the welfare and happiness of our brother-man and sister-woman identical with our own, and our duty to care, provide for, and assist them in their needs. The illustration is palpable to observation, and the duties of man to God and his fellow-beings clearly shown by the good Father in which true religion should be outwrought in human life.

But before we made the discovery that the two codes of Charges were different, that Anderson had in the 1738 Edition published a different code from that of 1723, some enlightened Masons in the United States, close investigators, who had *never seen a copy of the* 1738 *Constitutions,* but assumed, *believed* that all copies of the Ancient Charges published by order of the London Grand Lodge were uniform and verbatim copies of the 1723 Edition, and having a copy of Dermott's Ahiman Rezon, in which the Ancient Charges are word for word copies of the 1738 Anderson's edition, assumed that Dermott had made innovations, had altered the Ancient Charges, and called him for that reason an impostor, innovator, and other bad names, and even invaded the sanctity of his domestic life in vile vituperation, — all on the erroneous assumption that he had made changes in the Ancient Charges, which he did not do. What would have been the result, if the Charges had been applied to Anderson, as he was the guilty one? But the offence, if it was an offence, was not Anderson's alone, — the Grand Master and the members of the Grand Lodge sanctioned and approved the second code of Ancient Charges.

The question again recurs, "Why were the changes made? why adopt a different code of Ancient Charges from those approved and sanctioned by the Grand Lodge in 1723, and published in its Book of Constitutions?" It is singular that the Dermott copy of the Ancient Charges is verbatim the same throughout as the Anderson 1738 Code. Dermott was an Ancient York Mason, was Grand Secretary of the Grand Lodge at York, and his Ahiman Rezon was the Book of Constitutions of the York Grand Lodge, as all Ahiman Rezons are of the Grand Lodges which authorize their publication. We have no better opinion of Dermott's Ahiman Rezon than we have of Anderson's or subsequent Books of Constitutions published by authority of the London Grand Lodge. All of them were published under influences in derogation of the fundamental principle of Masonry, its universality and cosmopolitan character; and truth compels us to apply the same remarks to *all* publications of a like nature embracing the Ancient Charges as containing the fundamental laws of the Grand Lodges by whose authority they were published.

Although Dermott's Ahiman Rezon was published eighteen years after Anderson's 1738 ed., yet there are good reasons for believing that his Ancient Charges were not copied from Anderson, but had been the written code of the York Masons many years prior to 1738; and therefore the reason why Anderson published that code, and why the London Grand Lodge authorized its publication, in place of the 1723 code, are questions of great importance. And it is somewhat ominous that no one among the intelligent Masons of England has given this subject any attention, although some of the best minds are engaged in investigating and searching in every direction for glimpses of light on the early history of Masonry in England.

We have above given our opinion why the London Grand Lodge and Anderson adopted a new code of Ancient Charges in 1738. If we take into consideration that Ancient York Lodges existed in London in 1717; that before the formation of the London Grand Lodge there were many Masons who did not affiliate with the London Lodges, and kept up their organizations; that these Lodges did not unite in the formation of the Grand Lodge but continued under the York Grand Lodge Constitutions; that the London Grand Lodge was intent to have exclusive jurisdiction, therefore ignored the existence of the Mother Grand Lodge at York, and proclaimed its Masons seceders, irregular, schismatics, and finding

that after nearly two decades, having used every pos
sible means to compel the York Masons to come
under their banner without avail ; they resorted to the
plan of publishing the Ancient York code of Charges
as a means to accomplish their aim to induce the
York Masons to believe that they still adhered to the
Ancient Constitutions, Charges, and usages of the
fraternity.   But that ruse did not succeed, and after a
lapse again of eighteen years, the London Grand
Lodge in 1756 reverted back to the 1723 Charges,
the same year that Dermott published his first edition
of the Ahiman Rezon.

We have every reason to believe that the Ancient
Charges of Anderson were not the true, and for the
reasons set forth in the "Approbation" to the 1723
ed., wherein it is stated, " Whereas *the old Constitutions in England have been much interpolated, mangled,
and miserably corrupted*, not only with false spelling,
but even *with many false facts* and gross errors in
history and chronology," &c., and the Grand Master
" having ordered the Author to peruse, *correct and
digest, into a new and better method*, the history,
charges, and regulations of the Ancient fraternity ; he
has accordingly examined several copies from Italy
and Scotland, and sundry parts of England, and from
thence, (though in many things erroneous,) and from
several other ancient records of Masons, he has drawn
forth the above written *new Constitutions, Charges,
and General Regulations*.   These were submitted to
the late and present Deputy Grand Master to peruse
and correct, the Masters and Wardens of particular

Lodges, also the late Grand Master, when the same was ordered to be printed, and to which the present Grand Master, Grand officers, and Masters and Wardens," (with the consent of the Brethren and Fellows in and about the cities of London and Westminster,) having perused *the performance*, do join in the solemn approbation which *they believe will answer the end proposed;* all the valuable things of the old records being retained, the errors in history and chronology corrected, the false facts and the improper words omitted, and the whole *digested* in a new and better method. And they ordain these to be "the only Constitutions of free and accepted Masons amongst us."

Now we submit to the intelligent reader, after perusing the above statements taken from the *Approbation* to the 1723 Book of Constitutions, to which the Grand Master, Deputy Grand Master, Grand Wardens, and Masters and Wardens of *Twenty Lodges* affixed their signatures, if the whole or any part of this new "performance" ought to be accepted as a rule and guide, as containing the fundamental original laws, charges, usages of the fraternity of Masons, after the unwarranted declaration that the "old constitutions of England" had been much *interpolated, mangled, miserably corrupted* with *false spelling, false facts, gross errors*, out of which medley he, Anderson, compiled the new constitutions, charges, and general regulations.

How did the Grand Master or Anderson, or any of that revolutionary clique, know that the old constitutions had been interpolated, miserably corrupted?

Did they not antecedently work under that old constitution ? or had *they* since 1567 commenced altering, interpolating, and corrupting the old constitutions ? They certainly did not go back and reproduce the ancient documents. If they had continued to work under the old constitutions, they would not have differed from the York Masons. But in order to differ from them, and to give some plausible pretext for getting up a new *performance*, a new constitution, &c., they made those unwarranted statements set forth in the approbation. The unbiassed, thinking Mason, on reading no more than that approbation carefully, can surely come to no other conclusion than that there was some object back of all that is stated in order to give character to, or show a necessity for, the new production.

The Ancient Charges are believed to contain the fundamental principles, laws, and usages of the craft, and to have come down to us unmutilated, uncorrupted, unaltered ; at least so Masonic writers inform their readers ; and here in this 1723 Book, the author, as well as the Grand Lodge which authorized its publication, and to which it gave its legal sanction, tell us a different story and give us a new version, a compilation from vitiated and corrupt sources, as they themselves declare, as the Charges to be read at the making of Masons. But authors, to be true to themselves and consistent, ought to have good memories, which is applicable as well to Grand Masters as to all humans.

We see, in the above extracts copied from the 1723

Book of Constitutions, that the Masters and Wardens of *twenty Lodges* gave their approbation to the performance. The Lodges are *numbered* from one to twenty, *without names or places of meeting.*

Anderson reports in 1738 ed., at a meeting of the Grand Lodge, Sept. 29, 1721, he was ordered to digest the old Gothic Constitutions in a new and better method. On 27th Dec., 1721, the Grand Lodge "appointed fourteen learned Brothers to examine Bro. Anderson's manuscript." On 25th March, 1722, the committee of fourteen reported, "after some amendments had approved of it." On the *17th January*, 1723, "G. Warden Anderson *produced the new Book of Constitutions now in print, which was again approved,* with the antient manner of constituting a Lodge." We call attention to the date when the new Book was produced in print and approved by the Grand Lodge. We mention here that there are no proceedings of the Grand Lodge published in the 1723 ed. from its formation in 1717, except at the end of the Book a notice that "London, this 17th day of January, 1723, at the Quarterly Communication, *This Book . . . . . . was this day produced here in print,* and approved by the Society," signed by the Grand and Deputy Grand Masters.

Anderson, unfortunately for his reputation, has published in the 1738 edition "a list of the Lodges in and about London and Westminster," with the places of meeting and "dates of constitution" of each respectively in order. In that list, down to *March,*

1723, there were really only *ten Lodges constituted.*
In prefatory remarks to that list, Anderson says:
" Many Lodges have by accidents broken up, or are
partitioned, or else removed to new places for their
conveniency, and so, *if subsisting*, they are called and
known by those new places or their Signs. *But the
subsisting Lodges*, whose officers have attended the
Grand Lodge or Quarterly Communication, and
brought their benevolence to the general Charity
within twelve months past, are *here set down according to their seniority of Constitution, as in the Grand
Lodge Books and the engraven list.*"

Whatever there may be in these remarks, there
is too great a difference between *ten* subsisting lodges
at that time and *twenty-five Lodges being represented* January, 1723. One or both of these editions
must be false, yet Anderson was author of the two.
At the organization of the Grand Lodge, 1717, there
were *four* Lodges. June 24th, 1721, *twelve* Lodges
are mentioned. 29th September, 1721, *sixteen* Lodges.
27th December, 1721, *twenty* Lodges. 25th March,
1722, *twenty-four* Lodges, and 17th January, 1723,
twenty-five Lodges. What became of those other
fifteen Lodges? Were they *bogus* lodges? or were
they *broken up* " by accidents "? What kind of accidents? There can be no doubts about those on the
Grand Lodge Books and the engraven list, yet there
is a discrepancy here which no mathematician nor
logician can get over. The records of the Grand
Lodge show twenty-five lodges present, the Grand
Lodge Books show only ten constituted at that time.

There is certainly violence done to truth somewhere. The twenty Lodges whose Masters and Wardens approved of the 1723 New Book of Constitutions, if constituted lodges must have had a local habitation if not a name, why not mention either or both? Was it considered that the Book would not be examined closely, not criticised? It was an incautious remark of Anderson that "many lodges have by accidents broken up." That accords with a previous opinion we expressed and have long held, that the many who seceded or left the Lodges under the London Grand Lodge went over to the York Lodges.

As the York Grand Lodge was opposed to publishing anything pertaining to Masonry, as the London Grand Lodge manifested its hostility to that body of Masons by persistently ignoring its existence, and as it was constantly in trouble on account of the secession of its members, and annoyed at Lodges of York Masons being established in its midst, and at not having exclusive authority throughout the entire kingdom; it is a reasonable inference that the York Masons were quite numerous, and were increasing not alone from initiations in their lodges, but by accessions from those made under the London Grand Lodge banners. And it is no wonder that such should have been the case, as the York Masons had antiquity of constitution on their side, had not deviated from Ancient Masonic teachings, had not innovated upon the Landmarks nor the secret work, but adhered to the usages and ancient ceremonies of the fraternity. The London Masons, those under the

new Grand Lodge, have no such record.   Their innovating tendencies manifested in 1567, were continued
through subsequent years on many occasions; they
were under no consistent established authority.   The
sole aim of the London Grand Lodge was to be
esteemed the sole Masonic government in the kingdom, and to attain which it resorted to any and all
means to render itself popular among all classes of
people, and used every effort to crush out all Masonic
Lodges which did not render obedience to it.   The
reticence of the York Grand Lodge was detrimental to
it in some respects, but it saved it from the damaging
reputation which must ever follow Anderson and the
London Grand Lodge in publishing such strange,
anomalous and inconsistent works as the two editions
of the Book of Constitutions, by all intelligent readers
who will take the trouble to critically examine them.
There are no more credulous people in the world
than the masses of Freemasons; they accept everything as truth that pertains to Masonry, and to them
Anderson's Ancient Charges are veritable gospels.

   Taking advantage of the fact that the York Grand
Lodge never permitted anything to be published concerning Masonry, some intelligent Masons, close investigators and deep thinkers, have come to the conclusion, after much research, that there were no Lodges
of Ancient York Masons except the old Lodge at
York, and the existence of that Grand Lodge has been
disputed mainly on the ground that they could not
find any records of such an Institution ; whilst at the
same time they have themselves furnished corrob-

orative evidence of the fact, not only that there was such a Grand Lodge, but also Ancient York Lodges. But if no records existed at this time, that would not be sufficient evidence that no such organization did exist.   There is not one of the thirteen original States of this Union that can show a clear record from the time Masonry was first established within its borders, nay, not a clear record from the first establishment of its Grand Lodge.   The statement of the Grand Lodge of Massachusetts, that in 1733 Henry Price was appointed Provincial Grand Master of New England, is neither confirmed by original records of that Grand Lodge, the records of the Grand Lodge of England, nor by Anderson's Book of Constitutions published in 1738, nor subsequent authorized publications by the Grand Lodge of England; although they contain the names of all Provincial Grand Masters, with the places for which they were appointed, the appointment of Henry Price is nowhere mentioned, and yet the statement of the Massachusetts Grand Lodge has been universally accepted as true, and we could mention other like instances of the kind.   Prior to the Revolution few records were made, and only a few fragments of them are preserved.

We have many traditions, some plausible, some mythical, and even some of the existing records have been traced not to be original and to be interpolated with "false facts," as the veracious Anderson's Constitutions are interpolated with "false facts."

In the examination of Brothers Findel's and Hughan's valuable publications we find many notices,

rightfully interpreted, substantiating our views herein
expressed as to the continued existence of the York
Grand Lodge; and notwithstanding some papers apparently showing that the "Ancient Masons" formed
an independent Grand Lodge, making the third Grand
Lodge in England, they contain nothing to invalidate
our statements that they were Masons and lodges
holding under the York Constitution with the name
York omitted in the publications of the London Grand
Lodge, and Preston and others who copied from that
source. We would freely copy from Findel's "History of Freemasonry," and Hughan's "History of
Freemasonry in York," and "Unpublished Records
of the Craft," but in doing so we would be obliged to
make lengthy extracts, which with our comments on
them would so far exceed our limits as to duplicate
the number of pages in this small volume.

As we are unable to find, after long search, many
notes we had made on the *Ancient Regulations* adopted
by the London Grand Lodge in the 1723 ed., and
subsequent modifications of the same and adoption
of new ones to the period of the union, as well as
some comments from authors not referred to herein,
we may hereafter issue another volume, when we shall
review the books referred to of Brothers Findel and
Hughan. At the same time we commend to the Masonic Fraternity the two publications as being most
valuable and useful, and will be considered so in the
distant future by all intelligent reading Masons. And
we remark here that all the quotations and extracts
we have made from the 1723 and 1738 editions of

Anderson's Constitutions and Preston's Illustrations of Masonry, will be found in our reprints of two volumes of the " MASONIC LIBRARY."

In this review we are biassed by no prejudice, no hostile feeling, no other thought, than to give a right direction to the popular Masonic sentiment so long influenced by partial writers, whose Masonic publications were mainly intended to pervert truth in the interest of an Institution which it was their aim to represent as the only regular Masonic organization in England and the progenitor of the present Grand Lodge of England. The Masons under the London Grand Lodge were not a regular body of Masons; the Grand Lodge was not a legally constituted body; its organization was a usurpation of power to which it had no claim; it always had been subordinate to the York Grand Lodge; the concession of the latter body in giving them the appointment of a Grand Master for the South did not divide the jurisdiction; it was simply a privilege granted to the London Masons as a matter of convenience; and they continued to hold that subordinate position until the revolution. And during the time after the privilege was granted them to appoint a Grand Master for the South they manifested a rebellious spirit and usurped unauthorized powers which the Grand Lodge at York in a truly Masonic spirit overlooked. But the London Masons did not respond to the kindly Masonic spirit of the Parent towards its contumacious, seditious offspring, and continued insubordinate until the consummation of the Revolution. As a justification for their rebellious act they made the pretext that Sir Christopher Wren as Grand Master "neglected the Lodges," but they do not state the facts correctly, nor the cause. Sir Christopher had been Grand Master for a number of years, was appointed Deputy Grand Master in 1666, and occupied one or the other of these offices until 1710, and perhaps longer, as no Grand Master is mentioned until 1717. He was appointed Surveyor-General and principal Architect by the Crown in 1666, and continued to hold the positions until, in his nine-tieth year, in the full vigor of active life, he, through the influence of enemies, was displaced and William Benson, an inferior architect, "was made surveyor of the buildings, &c." Such an insult to one of his at-tainments and world-wide fame caused him "to de-cline all public assemblies," and the Master Masons in London, disgusted at the treatment of their old Grand Master, would not meet under the sanction of Benson, and "the Brethren were struck with a leth-argy which seemed to threaten the London Lodges with a final dissolution."

This shows that the London Masons under the Grand Master at the South were much disaffected, so that at the formation of the Grand Lodge there was not a sufficient number of Lodges to constitute a Grand Lodge, as it was then considered that not less than five lodges were necessary to form a Grand Lodge.

The York Masons were not affected by the demor-alized condition of the London craft otherwise than gaining members from the defection of the London body. Hence the small number of London Masons in 1717, at the time of the formation of the London Grand Lodge. The insufficient and incomplete statements of Anderson show a design to conceal and distort important facts and mislead the reader in regard to actual occurrences and the existing state of Masonry in England, from the commencement to the close of his Books of Constitutions.

We have already referred to the fact that Anderson in the 1723 ed. *is silent as to the organization of the Grand Lodge in* 1717. He does not mention it at all. It is only in the 1738 ed. that he gives a few particulars of that event. Why did he not give those few particulars, unsatisfactory and deficient as they are, in the 1723 ed., as the *Grand Lodge was then,* according to his statement, *in the sixth year of its existence ?* We can come to no other conclusion than that the story of the organization of the Grand Lodge in 1717 *is a fabrication,* was manufactured in the interval between 1723 and 1738. The manner in which the story is introduced in the 1738 ed. is sufficient to throw doubt upon the whole statement. Anderson was an active partisan in the revolution, and he was as well, if not better, acquainted with the facts of the organization of a Grand Lodge in 1723 than in 1738, if such Grand Lodge was formed in 1717. But there are other circumstances, omissions, and contradictions, which go far to prove, in connection with what we have already shown, that the story of the organization of the Grand Lodge in 1717 is a fiction, fabricated and invented by the Rev. Bro. Anderson. He mentions, as we have already stated, that *twenty* Masters and Wardens of Lodges gave their approval to the 1723 Book of Constitutions, when in his list of Lodges printed in 1738 he shows there were only *ten* Lodges constituted up to that time, January, 1723. He does not give the name of the mystical brother, "*the oldest* Master Mason, *now the* MASTER *of a Lodge*," nor the Lodge he was Master of; neither the names of those "some old Brothers" who with the four Lodges "constituted *themselves* a Grand Lodge *pro tempore* in due form." That oldest Master Mason then Master of a Lodge was put into the chair on that occasion, and his name ought to have been handed down to posterity, especially as Anderson *repeats*, at a subsequent meeting, when Mr. Antony Sayer, Gentleman, was by a majority of hands elected Grand Master of Masons, " the oldest Master Mason now the Master of a Lodge in the Chair."

Why, Bro. Anderson, did you not give the name of that oldest Mason Master of a Lodge, even if he was not a gentleman ? Why excite the curiosity of your brother Masons in all future time in withholding the name of that distinguished brother, the oldest Master Mason the Master of a Lodge, who was put in the chair at that revolutionary convention, and again at the inauguration of that new Grand Lodge ? By a few strokes of your pen you would not only have satisfied the curiosity of your brothers, but put to rest forever that constant repeated inquiry, "who was the oldest Mason ? " If, Brother Anderson, you had given the name of the Lodge that oldest Mason was Master of, it would have been some satisfaction, as that name could have been got from the Records; but you did no such thing, therefore the world must forever remain in darkness who that occupant of Solomon's chair was.

As Anderson is the only authority for the organization of a Grand Lodge in London, in 1717, as his statements are mingled with so much mystery and contradiction, and as he in 1723 ed. does not mention the formation of the Grand Lodge, then in the sixth year of its constitution, but waits until 1738, fully twenty years afterwards, before he gives the discrepant, contradictory, unreconcilable information, we are warranted in the belief that the entire statement was made up by Anderson and his co-revolutionists to justify themselves in cutting off all relations with the Mother Grand Lodge at York.

It must be remembered that prior to 1567 all the Masons in England derived their authority from the York Grand Lodge, and that at no period subsequent were the relations severed. The granting the privilege of selecting a Grand Master for the South did not affect the relations of the Masons in England; they were all under the banner of the Grand Lodge at York, that is, were Ancient York Free and Accepted Masons until the revolution in London, 1717; the London Masons, *affecting independency*, formed an independent Grand Lodge. As they were unmindful of their obligations prior to that time, as their own record proves, so they continued subsequently infringing every rule of propriety and right, and eventually

changing the ancient landmarks, and thus they became an illegal body of Masons.   And yet, with an
audacity that has no parallel in history, they assumed
to be the only legitimate body of Masons in England,
and pronounced all others as irregular.   It is true
they ranked amongst those under their banner kings,
princes, and the nobility, and men of high culture.
Yet it was no difficult matter to deceive them by false
representations, which they easily could do, as they
were the only Masonic body that had published anything relating to Masonry; and the character of their
publications we have only faintly noticed.   And truth
obliges us to admit, if the publications are a truthful
record of their benevolence and charity, they carried
out the chief of Masonic duties, the basic principle of
Masonry, Charity, an example worthy of imitation by
all true Freemasons, and which as a redeeming quality goes far as a set-off to their many derelictions
and departures from Masonic principles.

It was the exhibitions of their noble charities more
perhaps than anything else which attracted those in
high life towards the Masonic Institution, as benevolent and charitable actions always harmonize with
the generous sympathies of noble and true men.   It
is of no consequence if the charities of the London
Masons had the selfish aim of ostentation with the
view of commending themselves to the favorable consideration of the nobility, the object of relief to the
poor and needy was attained.

It is to be noticed that the distinctive terms Ancient and Modern Masons, Preston observes as being

applied by the irregular Masons in 1739, but neither Entick's nor Blaney's Books of Constitutions use the term Modern. As we have before stated, the term Modern was applied to the London Masons for changing the ancient usages, the distinguishing landmarks by which Masons everywhere recognized each other; but as the York Masons had not made any changes, but maintained and held to the ancient teachings, they very properly were entitled to be called Ancient, the title they had always held.

But Entick does not mention the Ancient Masons until 1755, and only *once*. But that Ancient York Masons and Modern Masons were terms applied to two different bodies of Masons in England there can be no doubt: the former title to those who had not departed from the Ancient Landmarks; the latter, to those who had. The two terms were in use until a very recent period, and may be yet in some places in instructing new-made Brothers in the mode of examination, and such instruction can be carried back to the beginning of the century, although at the union of the two bodies in England, 1813, the distinction ceased.

In connection with the subject of the union we make the following remarks, although we go back on a previous statement. When the Duke of Athol resigned as Grand Master of the Ancient York Masons in favor of the Duke of Kent, the latter stated, after his installation as Grand Master, "that he had accepted the office with the sole view of co-operating more effectually, *perhaps*, with his Illustrious Brother

of Sussex, in promoting and cementing the so much
desired Union." As the Duke of Kent was made a
Mason under the Ancient banner, he cautiously introduced the word " perhaps " in his remarks, reflecting
no doubt as to the difficulty in regard to which the
two bodies so essentially differed. It is possible that
that was the most important difference in the Masonry of the two bodies; and as one or the other
must change in order to effect a union, the *perhaps*
arose in his mind, *which ?* The Duke of Kent was no
doubt influenced by his Royal Brother, and the consequence of that influence is, that the Masons of Europe
and America, with the exception perhaps of some
parts of Germany, had entailed upon them the innovation of the London Masons in 1739, and strictly
Ancient Masonry ceased, and Modern Masonry was
adopted at the union.

Anderson's Constitutions as authority have always
been accepted as containing the Ancient Charges of
the craft; they have never been questioned; but if
we examine the circumstances under which they were
accepted and approved, and the condition of the fraternity subsequent to their adoption, a strong doubt
may well be entertained if they were unmutilated
copies of the Charges which the Masons were governed by before. It may, we think, be taken for
granted that those who formed the Grand Lodge in
1717 had but little knowledge what the Ancient
Charges were, and that is the view expressed by Dermott. At the meeting of that Grand Lodge on 24th
June, 1718, it was desired of the brethren " to bring

to the Grand Lodge any old writings and records concerning Masons and Masonry, *in order to shew the usages* in ancient times; and this year several old copies of the Gothic Constitutions were produced and collated."

The Grand Master the Duke of Montagu *found fault with all* the copies of the old Gothic Constitutions; he ordered Brother Anderson to digest the same in a new and better method, and at the desire of the Grand Lodge, 29th September, 1721, appointed fourteen learned Brothers to examine Brother Anderson's manuscript. At the Grand Lodge, 25th March, 1722, the Committee of Fourteen reported they had perused Brother Anderson's manuscript, &c., and after *some amendments* had approved of it, when he was ordered to have it printed.

What reliability can be placed upon a book as authority for the government of Masons as a rule and guide gotten up under such circumstances, and yet the large majority of Freemasons believe that the Constitutions, the Ancient Charges, as published by Anderson, have been the same from immemorial time. It would seem, from the statement that the old Gothic Constitutions had to undergo revision, that the Grand Master found fault with them, were amended by the committee, that some differences of opinion in regard to the Compilation existed among the craft at that time. And in examining the records from 1717 to 1813, the time of the union, we find, through all that period of nearly one hundred years, constant confusion, dissatisfaction, and discord among the Lon-

don Masons, caused no doubt in a great degree by
the departures of their Grand Lodge from the original
Constitutions.

Prior to the organization of the Grand Lodge in
1717, harmony existed among the fraternity in England, excepting the constant encroachments the London Masons made on the prerogatives of the York
Grand Lodge, which did not, however, interrupt fraternal intercourse, because the latter, like a kind
gentle mother, would not disturb the harmony of the
fraternity, but pursued the milder course of overlooking their exercising privileges belonging to her exclusively. But no sooner had these rebellious children
set up an independent government for themselves and
disowned their mother, than from the commencement
of the new establishment disaffection among themselves was manifested, disloyalty to the new regime
appeared, and its members were constantly leaving its
Lodges.

There is one feature about the Books of Constitutions authorized to be published by the London
Grand Lodge, and that is, they furnish no kind of sta-
tistical information; it would seem to have been designed intentionally to keep even their own members
in ignorance as to that kind of information. It is
much to be regretted that all the Books published by
its authority are so meagre on every subject, the details of its transactions are so minute, that they possess the smallest possible value to the investigating
student. If there were any means of arriving at a
knowledge of the proximate number of Lodges in

England and of their members, it would in some degree be a satisfaction. It would have been most important information, if we possessed a knowledge of the number of members of both bodies, to know the strength of each. And it is remarkable that no writer, not excepting Preston and Oliver, throws aside the veil so that we can have a glimmering of light on the subject. But more than all to be regretted is that at the union we are left in the dark as to their comparative strength; the subject is not mentioned, and yet it would appear that so important a matter on that eventful and much desired occasion, the number of Lodges at least on each side would have been stated. The only matter connected with the subject is, according to the articles agreed on for the union, the Grand Master of each Grand Lodge was to appoint nine expert Master Masons, and the eighteen experts were to form a " Lodge of Reconciliation." The names of these experts are mentioned separately, with the number of their Lodges set opposite their names. The highest number on the side of the London Grand Lodge is 453, and the highest on the York side is 244. But to the intelligent craftsman these numbers do not indicate the real number of working Lodges, as, when Lodges die out or for some cause are erased from the Grand Lodge Books, their numbers are not immediately filled up; succeeding Lodges are generally numbered upwards from the last on the list.

From the foregoing review the reader will at least have learned the lesson that when men depart from

a principle of right, from whatever motives, a condition of inharmony will naturally arise and disturbances
result which will render a return again to the right
direction most difficult.   The London Masons never
lost sight of their original aim to exclusive Masonic
rule throughout the kingdom, and with a persistence
worthy of a better cause left no means untried, but resorted to measures disgraceful to them as men, and
continued in their un-Masonic course, until some of the
most upright and intelligent among them determined
upon a change of conduct and advocated the necessity
of a union with the Ancient York Masons.   The first
impulse to that movement was given by the Prince of
Wales.   But the departures from the Ancient Landmarks by the London Masons were too widely dif-
fused and too strongly impressed upon the members
through long years of usage to be eradicated, hence
we have the evils originating with them entailed upon
us.   And, like the Oriental fable of Eve eating the
tempting fruit upon which all sectarian creeds hinge,
and upon which the popular sects predicate the dogma
of " original sin," &c., the evils originating with the
London Masons in the introducing sectarian symbols
and theologic illustrations in Masonic teachings, have
descended to their successors and are incorporated in
the Masonic system throughout the world.   Sectarianism is the opposite to Cosmopolitanism, and consequently has no affinity with Masonry.   Masonry,
Cosmopolitan Masonry, is the light and air thought
of the Universal Father.   Sectarianism is narrow in its
conceptions, clannish in organization, propagandive in

aim, and unprogressive in principle. Its introduction
into the Masonic system has caused Cosmopolitan
Masonry to be divested of its universality, of the
great principle illustrated in God's symbolism, and
diverted into a narrow and constantly narrowing
channel. The spiritual idea which underlies the
foundation of Masonry has been lost sight of, and the
materialism of theology generally obtains, as seen in
the productions of most of its popular teachers and
writers. The tendency towards a trinitarian theology
is rapidly advancing, and innovations in that direction
have been and are incorporated in approved Masonic
publications. The fact may be denied, but it is as
clear as the noonday sun ; and *the Masonic Book is not
published that does not prove our statement.* The introduction of sectarianism into Masonic teachings has
materialized the Masonic system, and the spiritual idea
is no longer recognized or taught.

A system, comprehending the Universal Father,
representing the several stages of human life, and the
beautiful phenomenon called death, progressing on-
wards to a higher life, in its spiritual significance
forms no part of Masonic teachings. The illustrations of modern teachers are in the main on the plane
of materialism and sectarianism commingled. The
spiritual is the ideal of Masonry ; its reality, and its
proper illustrations, are in a different direction from
that generally taught. The symbolism of God is not
taught in books, nor read in books, and yet His
symbolism, so clearly illustrated that all unbiassed intelligent minds can readily read, should be the com-

plement of Masonic teachings. God teaches through spiritual life, and teaches no other way. His illustrations through phenomenal nature and through man are the symbolisms given to our conscious perceptions, as the mode and manner of his teaching to the human kind. It is for us to read the symbolism aright, so that in instructing others we can impart the spiritual idea which each symbol teaches. As all Masons should be men of scientific acquirements, as their relations to the fraternity require they should be, it becomes a duty then to *demand* that all who desire to be made Masons should possess the scientific acquirements to comprehend the spirituality of God's symbolism illustrated in nature's phenomena, or God's works. It is through spirit life all forms in nature are outwrought through which man expresses his activities, mental and physical. All that we see, all nature, suns, planets, and worlds, and all within, around, and on them, are spiritual symbolic thoughts, *God's symbols formed of and through spirit-life.* The *subjective* reality ought therefore to form the basis of Masonic teachings, and not the *objective*, which is almost universally adopted. It is only the free intelligent mind that comprehends and realizes that man, although clothed in nature's habiliments in mundane life, is a spiritual being notwithstanding. The spiritual survives the material life. It is indestructible. It loses nothing by casting off, or being released from the exterior material form. Consciousness ever and eternally inheres in individual spirit-being, and in its progressive life, through higher

spheres through the eternal ages, it continues to unfold its divine spiritual individuality. We have only
briefly stated our view of what should be the nature
and character of Masonic teachings. If we take into
consideration that we claim to be a scientific Institution, that Masonry is a science embracing in its widest
sense all sciences, and that *the desire for knowledge
and to benefit our fellow-beings* are requirements that
applicants to learn our mysteries must possess; it is
evident that none but men of scientific culture were
intended to be invested with a knowledge of the mysteries of Masonry.

What evidence is there that Masonry is a scientific
institution ? Are there any exhibitions of it observa-
ble among the members of the fraternity ? Is our
claim a mere pretence ? Are none admitted among
the fraternity but men of scientific culture ? These
questions ought to be answered affirmatively, but in
truth cannot be. Masonry, instead of unfolding pro-
gressively with the intellectual advancement of scientific knowledge and general intelligence, has departed
from the original aims of the fraternity, and is apparently inclining towards a sectarian society. That is
plainly to be seen, not only from 'the close, and constantly drawing closer, relations with Templarism,
and also the persistent determination *not to expunge*
the sectarian innovations, interpolated in the ritual
from Masonic teachings; but the increasing efforts to
popularize the institution in many ways, and in erect-
ing extravagant edifices out of means that should be
devoted to charitable purposes in the relief of poor

and needy brethren, and widows and orphans of de-
ceased Masons. These are all the natural outgrowths
of theologic institutions influenced by a general sentiment in that direction, and are inheritances coming
down through the past century from the actors of
that period, who in departing from Masonic principles
transmitted their tendencies, which their descendants
have amplified to a very great extent. The tendency
to innovate and interpolate in Masonic teachings has
taken a wide scope since the great Masonic charlatan
of the United States, Thomas Smith Webb, commenced his Masonic career, near the close of the last
century. Since then the Ancient and Accepted Scottish Rite has grown vastly in this country and elsewhere. This offshoot of legitimate Freemasonry, as
well as Webb's new degrees and other interpolations,
which have become incorporated in the Masonic system, are in contravention of the catholic, cosmopolitan principles of Ancient Freemasonry. The new
degrees of Webb, and his corruptions of Masonic
teachings, have been introduced in most jurisdictions in the United States; and although known that
they did not form any part of Ancient Masonry, yet
they were approved the same as legitimate, and are
worked under legal authorized warrants. It would
appear that the Masonic fraternity of this country are
as indifferent to the ancient landmarks and usages of
Masonry as the Masons in the past century under the
London Grand Lodge were; also, as if the autonomy
of Grand Lodges was inadequate to the preservation
of principles inherent in them as the custodians of

legitimate Masonry. In them resides the power of self-government; and if exercised as it should have been, we would not have the fungous excrescences of unnatural degrees and systems of so-called Masonry diverting the attention of the craft from the original system of Masonry. We can only regret that every Grand Lodge did not imitate the example of the United Grand Lodge of England in establishing the principle that *Masonry consists of three degrees* ONLY, *including the Royal Arch*, and it would have been better if the Royal Arch had been returned where it was originally, and from which it was taken — the Master's degree. But innovation and accumulation of degrees have been rampant, to gratify a perverted taste for novelty; and an insatiate curiosity for "higher degrees" seems never will be appeased. The cause of this vitiated taste and undue curiosity is not difficult to solve. It is clear to every thinking mind, and has frequently been adverted to. The true cause is in admitting persons into the fraternity who not only do not possess the requisite qualifications, but whose animus of desire to become Freemasons is most generally on the lower plane of human life. The degrees are taken without the ability, in many cases, to comprehend the import of the lessons imperfectly given, and consequently the teachings are but faintly impressed upon the candidate.

The character of applicants can generally be known by those who recommend them; but that makes no difference, as generally they are considered "good fellows" by the recommenders, and in most cases

there is no further investigation.   It is this class of
men who have mainly populated our lodges in recent
years, and who, before the faint impression of the
Master's degree is removed, apply for other degrees,
pass through them in quick succession, which con-
fuses the candidate, so that long before the Royal
Arch is reached, the recollection of the symbolic lessons has faded from the mind, all but those important for social purposes, the manual signals of recognition.   There may be an excuse for lodges accepting
imperfect material, in Grand Lodge necessities, but
otherwise no contingency can possibly arise in the
Masonic needs of subordinate lodges, unless in ex-
tremely rare cases.

The quality of Masonry is generally in an inverted
degree to its popularity.   The external appearance is
no evidence, unless in the established character of
men well known for uprightness and integrity, and
none but such should be admitted into our lodges.
External show and parades, which never should be
allowed, are no signs of *real* prosperity.   They are
intended to catch the vulgar eye and influence such
to a favorable view of Masonry.

Neither are magnificent edifices signs of prosperity.
Intelligent men will reason with themselves, " Does a
charitable institution need such an expensive establishment?" "How were the means acquired?" "If for
charitable purposes, those who are the recipients of
the charities of the institution must have been limited,
and to their detriment, or perhaps neglected altogether."   Intelligent men will reason, and no doubt

such thoughts as we have expressed have arisen in many minds.

The thought comes, if the present popularity of Masonry is continued for a few years, and the rush to our portals and influx of members is continued of the material referred to, what will Masonry then be? We have our fears that true Cosmopolitan Masonry will only be known in history if the large increase of membership is continued and the tendency to become a sectarian society is not arrested; and in entertaining these fears we are by no means alone.

Freemasonry, in its original aim, was to establish a Universal Brotherhood, without distinguishing nationalities, throughout the race, and as a basis eschewed all opinions and beliefs, which had always caused antagonisms among men. The effort to attain that end which could only be accomplished in long series of years, was to associate men of high culture, moral integrity, and benevolent dispositions, with the object, by example, to imbue their fellow-men with the consideration that their happiness in this life lay in their moral improvement and progressive elevation to higher planes of thought and conduct. It was essential, therefore, to illustrate properly the aim of the association that none should be offered as exemplars whose lives were not in harmony with that aim. The exemplary life was the first consideration, if established from early youth. Not as propagandists, nor as reformers, did they undertake to carry out their views; only as their example influenced their fellowmen.

Within this brief statement we give the basis of Masonic association. Its origin is not to be traced any more than the original conception of any thought. It may have developed out of the Egyptian, Eleusinian, Dioclesian, or other ·ancient mysteries, or the builders or stonemasons. We do not believe in the Solomonian theory any more than the 1717 origin. Associations do not spring into being at once. There must have been a conception long maturing into a thought; and that thought, unfolding in centuries, matures the conception on the plane of intelligence, the needs of the time demand. The true origin of everything is in the primal conception, the germ which unfolds and develops, as all things in nature unfold from a germ and develop to maturity. But a thought never matures, because perfection is not possible to finite being. It however continues through the eternal ages to develop, as the interior perceptive faculties unfold. There is, therefore, a germ of truth in all the projected theories of the origin of Freemasonry.

Freemasonry is continually being modified in some direction or other. It has undergone many changes in the third of a century since we received the degrees of Masonry. Thought is never stationary. As with Freemasonry, so it has been with the so-called religious systems. All have developed out of a crude original conception, a common germ developed according to the conditions, times, and planes of human intellectual unfoldment. It has been the same with arts, science, philosophy, jurisprudence, governments, and social systems, obtaining in differing nations and races; all are the outgrowths of a primal conception, unfolded in the infancy of intellectual development. The basic principle of a germinal thought ever remains in all the outgrowths of development. The origin of no thing can ever be traced. The mind, in its efforts at exhaustive investigation, will necessarily be arrested by the limitation of the interior faculties or the incapacity of the mind to receive the impressions; and relief can only be found in the conclusion that all things have their origin in the infinite mind which by universal acceptance mankind agree in naming God.

Inductive reasoning necessarily commences where deductive reasoning ends, as to trace from the primal effort in producing phenomena is beyond the capacity of the finite mind; yet the deductive investigation advances, step by step, until its progress is seemingly arrested, but the investigation does not stop. It is, and ever will be, pursued by active, intelligent minds, seeking primal original causes. Truth is the aim of all honest inquiry. *Truth is a unit*, existing only in the Infinite, and towards the Unit truth all true investigations tend, whatever the subject or object of inquiry may be. That is a truth scientists have yet to learn; but confined in the range of their investigations to traditional authority, they limit the scope of their inquiries in accord with theologic conceptions of the Originator and moving Cause and unfolder of nature and material phenomena. All development of mind ever tends towards the unit thought. In the

ultimate all things are a unit, that is, a *dual unit*. A
single does not exist, and cannot.   It does not follow
that because a so-called Elementary, Primary cannot
be reduced, that it is not a compound.   There can be
no form, no force, light, heat, no thing that is a simple
elementary.   Nothing can exist that is not formed,
outwrought of the dual unit principle.   Webster, in
his definition of Elementary, is at fault, notwithstanding he accepts the views of the scientists.

The study of man and phenomenal nature properly
comes within the scope of Masonic investigations.
They should form the chief of Masonic teachings, to
lead the minds of the members from the frivolities
which generally engage their attention, and occupy
their thoughts to higher considerations and higher
conceptions of God.   Masonry should be considered
the all, the complement of science, because man is
the subject, and man is what concerns Masonry. The
study of man has always been considered the chief of
studies.   It is the most important, because man is the
co-worker with God in the advancement of the race,
in civilization, in improving the conditions to higher
attainments to benefit mankind.

In this progressive age, of all institutions and
associations, Masonry ought to be in the advance
in unfolding and disseminating intelligence, and
giving light on all subjects important and interesting
to their fellow-men.   But where shall we find this
important progressive knowledge?   It is not in print,
in authorized or unauthorized publications; these are
mainly written in the same style and train of thought

as the publications in England in the past century we have referred to, laudatory of principles of Masonry and the increasing prosperity of the institution, as the increase of members and increase of funds are considered. There are some exceptions to that broad statement in regard to authorized, but none that we can remember of unauthorized Books on Masonry.

If we look for progressive light in the primary departments, the subordinate lodges, we look in vain. The Masters have not generally the ability, if they had the disposition; and if they had both, the time is not at their command. The influx of applicants absorbs all the time in conferring degrees, which must be done rapidly, and much must of necessity be omitted; and it is not only fatiguing, but the mind of the Master cannot be sufficiently concentrated to perfect his work as it should be done. This condition of things arises from the assumed prosperity and the popularity inaugurated by the fraternity, bringing money into the treasuries and accession of members to lodges. The introduction of imperfect material, and the necessity of instructing candidates imperfectly, are evils that cannot fail to injure most materially the institution. But that which is of more importance is that the spiritual significance of Masonic illustration is not taught, and hence the teachings are devoid of those lofty inspiring sentiments which touch the mind and heart, and become deeply impressed upon the consciousness.

We consider Freemasonry the best institution, in its original principles, that the reason and intellectual development of man has ever conceived. It had its basis in the rights of man, the liberty of the individual, the dignity of labor, the recognition of the unity of the race, and the aim through progressive education, enlightenment, and civilization, to promote the elevation of man to a higher status of manhood, and a purer, truer conception of the divinely formed human being, and of the Divine Unfolder of the Universe. No institution or association of men was ever founded upon such noble benevolent designs, in promoting the culture and welfare of the race, and by humanizing efforts to elevate their thoughts to higher conceptions of their own being and their mission through the eternal future life. The design was of a far loftier character than any theology teaches or ever taught. Its consistent, practical, and ultimate attainments have never been eliminated or reached by any known system of ethics for man's guidance and rule of conduct. Its principles, free from all mystery, and acceptable to the understanding and conscience, have been intermixed by charlatans and designing teachers with creedal dogmas, in agreement with orthodox religionist tenets, with the aim to render Masonry acceptable to believers, and to popularize the Institution.

We acknowledge the efforts to have been effective, as the reports of committees on the sectarian question, approved by the Grand Lodges of New York and Massachusetts, and the general ritualistic teachings in Masonic lodges, prove. And that the reports were approved by these two Grand Lodges,

shows the dominant influence of sectarianism, which·
is greatly on the increase since Templarism has been
engrafted as a "higher degree," and which as a means
of deception has been destructive of the cosmopolitan
character of Masonry, and inconsistent with every
principle of the Masonic institution.   Masonry is no
longer *Free*, in its original sense, as a cement of union
to good and true men of every religious opinion ; only
in the narrow and perverted sense embraced in the
inconclusive and illogic views of the reports of the
committees referred to.

It is greatly to be lamented that men of biassed, of
intolerant dispositions, were ever admitted into Masonic Lodges, as history in all the past proves that
such were ever inimical to the peace and good order
of society, and therefore were, from the very nature
and design of Masonry, excluded from admission into
the fraternity.   To the Reverends Desaguliers and
Anderson, in introducing sectarianism into the body
of Masonry, we trace all subsequent innovations of
that character, which ultimating in a color of recognition of Templarism, as in the order of higher degrees of Masonry, its proper universal feature is only
referred to to deceive the ignorant.   Masonry and
Templarism are opposites, as discord and harmony,
peace and war, right and wrong, light and dark, good
and evil, which the obligations, the teachings, working
tools and implements clearly show, as well as the
qualifications required to become a Knight Templar.

We have been impelled from necessity to express
our views in regard to innovations, tending to subvert

the very foundation of Masonry, strongly, deter-
minedly, and reproachfully.   The times demand it,
because of the general depreciation of Cosmopolitan
Masonry — nay, ignoring it practically, — and because
of the general desire to be known as a *high* Mason,
and because of the undue ambition, so generally entertained, to acquire official position; and lastly, because all of these growing evils so plainly manifest,
those in high places holding the highest positions, in
their annual communications, in place of, with very
rare exceptions, noticing the tendency and drift of
these evils and the ultimate result to the Institution,
overlook them as if they did not exist.   Their expressions are mostly confined to flattering the feelings of the craft, in lauding in flowery and glowing
sentiments the beauties of Masonry and the excellence
of its principles, which, understood properly, are
mainly severe sarcasms of what should be, and not
intended as what is.   It is true much is said against
intemperance, profanity, gambling, &c., all of which
evils are the natural results of the imperfect material
so largely brought into the Masonic Temple.   But
there never should have been a necessity for mentioning that these evils exist among the fraternity;
and if the qualifications which Masonry requires of
applicants had been strictly observed, there would be
no need of mentioning them at all.   As they do exist,
the mere statement and inefficient action will not
eradicate the vices.

The only remedy, and the true one, is " to revert to
the ancient Landmarks," as the London Masons were

compelled to, and revert to the high standard of qualifications Masonry demands, which the antecedent life of applicants must have proved. That step, and that alone, will be a sure guarantee that the drunkard, the gambler, and the profane will not be found within the Masonic Temple. It is no excuse whatever, as is often remarked, that these vices exist in the Church. Masonry is founded upon widely different principles. It has a code of rules of its own. It is not the handmaid of religion, as the religionists among us frequently assert. Its true mode, in the strict sense, is to unfold the God in man. Not according to any *ism*, to any church creed, but by the exemplification of a divine life, in doing good, in helping and assisting his brother man, formed in the likeness of God, to improve his moral status, to illustrate in his actions that he is a child of God, to obey his interior divine impulses, and by subordinating his animal nature, to progress onward and upward to a higher sphere, to the spiritual, in view of the eternal life before him.

True Freemasonry has no system of faith or belief; its object is human elevation, in all that is necessary to that attainment. Its aim is practical, and not a belief which may be right or wrong. *Belief* is not *knowing*, but doing good, and acting right towards our brother man is the only way to "walk with God."

If we take into consideration that God is only known as he is manifested in and through his works, and that man is the ultimate and the chief of his creation, it is only through the activities of the human

being that God is known.   And as human beings
unfold their interior divine natures, the possibilities
existing within them, they become co-workers with
God in improving the race and improving the phenomena in nature, through intelligent action in elim-
inating the possibilities existing in nature.   Man,
through his intelligence, has improved the physical
forms of animals, of vegetables, fruits and flowers,
showing that the possibilities exist in him and in
nature ; but nature cannot improve unless it is
directed by the intelligent human being.   All the
advances in civilization, in every direction, whereby
humanity has been benefited, has been made through
efforts unfolding, bringing out, the possibilities in the
human being.

These sparks of scientific thought come properly
within the province of Masonic teachings. But teaching alone is not sufficient.   Every human being has
a capacity for something which should be cultivated
with all the intelligence man can bring to bear upon
it ; and just in the degree he does he will unfold his
interior possibilities.   The mode of God's manifestations is visible throughout the universe, and is ever
and ever teaching humanity, through material phenomena, unfoldment. Barren ground will not bear fruit.
The indolent man is not a producer. Man was made to
exercise his faculties, according to his best capacity,
to promote his own welfare and to benefit his fellow-
men. He should be a producer, as God intended
him to reciprocate, in some way, for that which he
consumes. All men should be producers, as all are

consumers. There is, therefore, an interrelation and dependence among and between all men. Man was not made for himself alone. Useful employment is practical devotion to the Supreme Being. If Masonic teachings were on the high plane they should be, Masonry would rank as a scientific institution — a school embracing all sciences, as some writers have claimed it to be.

Let us hope that the time is not distant when scientific instruction will be adopted, — when intelligent, unbiassed *free* minds will give a direction to remove the corruptions, the innovations, and false conceptions so largely interwoven in the Masonic ritual; and a higher — the highest qualifications demanded as absolute to a knowledge of the mysteries of Masonry.

It is a fundamental principle of Ancient Masonry that applicants for its mysteries *shall be* "good and true" men, and *not* that they shall, or may, *become* such *after* they have been admitted into the fraternity. As we have already remarked, Freemasonry is not a reformatory association; therefore, the knowledge must be conclusive that applicants *are*, in the fullest sense, *good and true* men *before* their application is acted on. The two terms must be taken conjointly, as expressive of perfect, upright man, in the widest application of the words.

In not seeking for the qualifications which Ancient Masonry demands, the standard was lowered, to the great injury of Masonry, and the consequent result was, that departures from its original design followed in interpolations and innovations, which have changed its character and given it a direction contravening its fundamental principles and the primary object and aim of the institution. It is generally admitted that much of the material brought into the Masonic Temple is too imperfect to be used in its construction; altogether unsuited to be wrought in the constructing of the moral edifice. A return then to original principles is demanded. A strict adherence not to admit within the portals of the institution, for the sake of friendship, or any other considerations, those who do not come up to the standard Masonry requires; who have not proved themselves to be good and true men in their conduct and intercourse with their fellow-beings, and as, in the motive expressed to become a Mason, "a desire of knowledge and to benefit their fellow-men," was the object, was not clearly manifested in their antecedent lives.

Let the heart and soul of all Freemasons be then directed to a return to original principles. Admit no applicants into the moral structure of Freemasonry whose lives are not in accord with the grand design of the GREAT OVERSEER; those who by the tests of the Plumb, Level, and Square, in their moral significance, are not upright, good, and true men. Glorious will be the advent of that determination. Its ultimate results will be that Masonry will rank high above all other institutions and associations of men, and its light will so shine, through the exemplary divine life of its membership, that there will be no need to laud the institution, to gratify the fraternity, nor to seek the world's popularity. May the eventful day arrive

when the benign and beneficent aims of Masonry will
be clearly manifest, that its influences will pervade the
world of mankind, inducing them to a higher culture
of individual life, a higher civilization, a closer fraternity, and peace and good will truly prevail throughout the world. Great and glorious will be that consummation, and let us pray, So mote it be.

We close with remarking that it is our decided
opinion that the union would not have been formed
if it had not been for the intelligent and unbiassed
views of the Prince of Wales, the patron of Freemasons in England. His mind was not cramped by the
narrow views and little ambition of the leading
London Masons. He had a higher regard for Truth
than an equivocal title to origin of institutions. His
noble soul was not confined within the narrow
bounds of those who preceded him as Grand
Master. He appears to have studied well the causes
of the differences existing among the Masons in his
kingdom, and, true to the instincts of his noble nature
and his intelligent and benevolent good heart, he rose
above those petty prejudices that inspired the London
Masons for nearly a century, and which he manifested
in the most magnanimous manner, in expressing that
*his "arms would ever be open to receive all the Masons
in the kingdom indiscriminately."* We hear him utter
no equivocal untruthful remarks, nothing to embitter
feelings nor to excite animosities, such as the London
Masons had continually manifested at their communications and in their publications. In that brief
remark he expressed more wisdom and Masonic jus-

tice than in all that was said or written by the
London Masons in the prior eight decades.   Indeed
it formed the germ which ultimated in the union.   It
would seem that the Duke of Athol accepted it as a
basic principle on which to found an agreement, without prejudice or loss of dignity or principle to the
Masonic fraternity, over whom he had presided for a
period of twenty years.   He had confidence in the
Prince of Wales that no injustice would be done, no
wrong in favor of either side in the details of arrangement for a union, but that everything would be conducted in a true Masonic spirit and on Masonic principles, and that no compromise of honor would be
expected or demanded.   In such belief he resigned
his position as Grand Master, and nominated the
Duke of Kent as his successor, whom he well knew,
being an Ancient York Mason, would not enter into
any agreement compromising the honor or dignity of
the Masons of whom he was Grand Master.

The remark referred to of the Prince of Wales no
doubt had its effect upon the London Masons, as we
find them taking the necessary preliminary steps towards a union with a body of Masons who had made
no changes in the secret work of the institution; by
the Committee of Charity, submitting a proposition,
which the Grand Lodge approved, April 12th, 1809,
by passing a resolution enjoining the several lodges
"to revert to the Ancient Landmarks of the Society,"
and to carry which into effect the Lodge of Promulgation was appointed.   This Lodge was supported by
subscriptions from the Lodges, and it was composed

of many members, and only such as were well acquainted with the Ancient Landmarks. And as much
time was necessarily employed in carrying out the
intent of the resolution, without remuneration, and as
it could not be expected that the members could give
their time and attention to a subject of such importance as teaching all of the Masons what the true
Landmarks were, therefore the Grand Lodge recommended the Lodges to continue the subscriptions
until the expenses of the Lodge of Promulgation were
discharged.

In the "Articles of Union between the two Grand
Lodges of England," the Duke of Kent has the pre-
cedence as "Grand Master of Free and Accepted
Masons of England, *according to the Old Institutions*,"
"on the one part," and the Duke of Sussex, as "Grand
Master of the Society of Free and Accepted Masons
under the Constitution of England," "on the other
part;" which corroborates in language, position, and
expression, the views herein given that the Grand
Lodge at York had a continued existence according
to the old institutions, down to the time when it
united with the London Grand Lodge in forming a
Grand Lodge under one Grand Master for the whole
of England. The union took place in 1813, when the
title of the United Grand Lodges became, THE UNITED
GRAND LODGE OF ANCIENT FREEMASONS OF ENGLAND.

ADDENDUM.

On page 99, the law enacted April 10th, 1777, would seem to have been passed for the purpose of forbidding the Masons under the London Grand Lodge from being present at the Conventions or meetings of the so-called Ancient Masons; and also forbidding their admittance into their Lodges "without being remade," from which we conclude that the members of both sides fraternized and visited each other's Lodges, without noticing their being regular or irregular. And from the frequent mention of irregular Lodges, and passing resolutions interdicting intercourse with irregular made Masons, or meeting with them in their Lodges, by the London Grand Lodge, it would appear that such resolutions and enactments were disregarded by many of its members, and that their visiting the irregular Lodges was continuous. But there is no mention of a single "irregular" "Ancient" Mason being "remade," which, if there had been, the London Grand Lodge would have noticed the fact, and magnified each one tenfold. The York Grand Lodge is not mentioned in that law, nor any reference to it, as, in other *exceptions* of censures, in which it is named in connection with Scotland and Ireland. The law reads "the persons who assemble in London and elsewhere," the elsewhere meaning the city of York and other places where York Lodges held meetings, and therefore the omission of the York Grand Lodge in the exemption from censure. That omission is a clear proof that the York Grand Lodge was the body under whose authority the so-called "irregular lodges" held their constitutions, and who were called Ancient Masons.

At page 106, the Earl of Moira, in his speech before the

Grand Lodge in Edinburgh, in speaking of the "irregular Masons" in England, remarks, "with whom *he under-stood* the Grand Lodge of Scotland had established an intercourse." We have already commented on that speech, and request the reader to turn back again and re-read the Earl's remarks. He says, *he understood*, &c., as if he had, as the Acting Grand Master of the Grand Lodge of England, only recent information of the fact. That speech was made in 1803, and the intercourse between the Grand Lodge of Scotland and the Grand Lodge at York had existed for many years; and, in 1772, as showing the fraternal intercourse between them, the Duke of Athol, who was Grand Master elect of the Grand Lodge of Scotland, was elected Grand Master of the Ancients — the Ancient York Masons — and continued to hold that position until 1813. Of all of these facts the Earl of Moira must have had knowledge, and he must have *known* — not understood — that the Grand Lodge of England, on April 10th, 1777, (see page 108,) took action against the "Ancient Masons," under "the patronage of the Duke of Athol." Therefore the Earl of Moira did not express the truth in his speech before the Grand Lodge at Edinburgh. The Earl of Moira was a strong partisan of the London Grand Lodge, and un-Masonic and uncharitably vindictive against the York Masons, styling them, indiscriminately, seceders, irregular Ancients, but never giving them their proper title, Ancient York, as the name York had been long before tabooed by the London Grand Lodge. But the liberal and unconditional view of the Prince of Wales expressed to the Earl of Moira as to the Masons *throughout* "the kingdom *indiscriminately*" caused him to change his course of action, and pursue the only proper course to attain a union with the Ancient York Masons, which the London Masons so much desired; that was "to revert again to the Ancient Landmarks of the Society." Every student in Masonry knows what that means, and that it was the Masons under the London Grand Lodge who had changed the Landmarks; but from some cause or other the change to the Ancient Landmarks was not complete. It may have been that the York Masons in and near London, in their frequent intercourse with the London Masons, were so indoctrinated with the innovation, that at the union their influence, added to the body of London Masons, may have prevailed in adopting "the right to the left and the left to the right," and transmitting the change through future Masonic teachings.

At page 122, last paragraph, Oliver mentions "the Ancients after their secession," held their meetings "without acknowledging a superior until 1772," when the Duke of Athol was chosen Grand Master. That is written in the Oliverian style, in the interest of the London Grand Lodge. He would make it appear that from 1739 to 1772 there were no Lodges in England of York Masons, and that those who seceded from the London Lodges were without a Grand Master, and consequently held meetings for thirty-one years without any warrant of authority. The statement is certainly ridiculous on its face. It is true we do not know who preceded the Duke of Athol as Grand Master. But as the Duke held the position of Grand Master of Scotland, it cannot be reasonable to believe that he would accept the position of Grand Master of an unorganized body of Masons in England. The intelligent Masons and members of the Grand Lodge of Scotland would not have permitted the dignity of the office to such humiliation. The object of the London Grand Lodge was to mystify the whole subject in reference to York Lodges and the seceders from its Lodges, and it had pliant tools in the publishers of the Books of Constitutions and Preston, and Oliver, who was its subsequent mouthpiece. But notwithstanding all that was said and done, the desire on the part of the London Masons for a union with those Ancients was strong and continued until they were forced to take the first movement towards its accomplishment. On same page (122), last line, Oliver continues the subject, and says, "This venerable nobleman," referring to the Duke of Athol, "*we may presume*, was convinced by the Royal Duke's arguments," &c., "how desirable must be an actual and cordial union of the two societies under one head." The reader cannot fail to have perceived that through all the transactions of the London Grand Lodge which we have noticed, the Ancients, seceders, irregulars, are all mentioned as outlaws and outcasts, in the most offensive manner, and by no means in a kindly or cordial spirit referred to before the Lodge of Promulgation was appointed. And consequently no effort was made to a reconciliation, even so late as the Earl of Moira's speech in Grand Lodge after his return from Edinburgh. All of which goes to prove that the London Grand Lodge strove to gain its end as the only Masonic authority in England to the very last, by persecuting and other un-Masonic acts, in hopes either to get the Ancients, irregulars, and seceders to disband their Lodges, or to absorb them under its Constitutions. And it also proves that the York Masons, to whom the offensive titles were applied, were strong enough to maintain their organization, would not recognize the Masons under the London Grand Lodge as Ancient Masons, therefore had no desire to form a union with them, and did not consider the subject until after the appointment of the Lodge of Promulgation, which was April, 1809. It was not the persuasion of the Royal Duke which inclined the Duke of Athol to a union, but the fact that the London Masons were compelled by the appointment of the Lodge of Promulgation by official authority, *to revert again to the Ancient Landmarks of the Society.* That action, and the expression of the Prince of Wales, who had the confidence of the York Masons, induced them to unite in forming a Grand Lodge under one head.

As we have referred on several occasions to Templarism, in the course of our writing, we deem it to be just to the reader, as well as to ourself, to give our views in regard to that institution and its assumed relation to Freemasonry, although our opinions have heretofore appeared in print, and we believe are known to the fraternity generally. We have no more objection to Templarism than to any other so-called religious organization; nay, less, for reasons we will advance. We object to any claim of relation with or to Freemasonry. We believe that claim has been detrimental to both institutions. Templarism is not Masonry, and never was so considered by intelligent Sir Knights. The presumed relation in requiring its applicants to be

Freemasons has been detrimental to it in preventing many good Christian men averse to Masonry, and many Masons, from joining their ranks who otherwise would if *it was a distinct and separate organization.* We have satisfied ourself on that point in a large intercourse with the clergy and members of Christian churches. As a separate organization, Templarism would be more widely known and would have a larger field to carry out its aims in any humanizing and benevolent efforts. Our objections are not to Templarism, *per se,* as a religious order. We favor any and all organizations whose objects are to care, provide for, and relieve the poor and needy; and in that high and noble aim Templarism in recent years has shown in its benevolences a humanizing spirit commendable in a high degree. In our aims and pursuits we are practical, and favor any association which practically demonstrates its principles in aiding its fellow-beings in times of need. It is in that view that we have considered the subject at all; and we have long been convinced that the relation of Templarism to Masonry has been injurious to each. Templarism has been detrimental to Masonry in its influences in a sectarian direction; and its relation to Masonry has been injurious in confining its membership to the Masonic fraternity, thus preventing many of the best class of Christians from coming into their association. If the Templar bodies would sever their connection with Masonry, and not make Masonic relation a qualification, and raise their standard high, they would soon become the leading organization in the civilized world. A presumed relation of the two different organizations has existed for many years. But the great American Masonic charlatan, Thomas Smith Webb, after engrafting the views of his innovations into the body of Masonry, then circumscribed the area of Templarism by engrafting into the Templar Constitution the qualification that applicants must be Royal Arch Masons. That the Templar organizations have submitted to the dictation and authority of Webb is a matter not easily explained, as the whole of his Masonic career was employed in fabricating new degrees, and interpolating, all for the sake of popularity to gain official position, and to be considered the leading mind in the fraternity of Masons.